Dating and Other Things Catholic

What Seminary Taught Me about Single Life

John Antonio

John Antonio

Edited by Anna Reynolds

ISBN-13: 978-1535370561

ISBN-10: 1535370564

"Life is like arriving late for a movie, having to figure out what was going on without bothering everybody with a lot of questions, and then being unexpectedly called away before you find out how it ends."

–Joseph Campbell

This book is dedicated to those who got a late start.

Contents

Acknowledgements

Special thanks to my parents for the gift of life, to my 9 brothers and sisters for helping me enjoy it, to the Gutierrez family for helping me chase the dream, to Trish and David Nevarez, my patient blog editors, to Fr. Christopher for teaching me to pray, to Ralph for turning me into a fighter, to Bernardo for being fascinated with my failings, to my friends Vince, Dana, Juliana, Heather, Kristin, Katie, Emily, Leah, James, Paul, Miguel, and David for their enriching conversations and insights.

From Seminary to Single Professional

The single years can be a confusing time in life. I define "single" as that period in which you are eligible to be married but are, of course, not yet married. This may vary according to individuals, but it often comes after college. You have a career in the works; you can support yourself financially and may even spend extra on someone special. You can dedicate energy and resources to building your life, finding a supportive community of friends, a place to live and a satisfying long-term career. You are more capable of developing a serious, stable relationship.

The demography of single people is growing, mainly because more people are living longer in a single status. In recent years the median age for marriage in many regions of the United States has jumped from 23 to 30 years. People are getting married later. Within this diverse demography, there exist many Catholics who work, date, build relationships, relocate, wake up, jog, go out, and start over. They repeat the cycle of single life over and over and spend a lot of time just figuring it out.

All this is exciting, but not easy. As a young Catholic, one may find oneself fresh out of college faced with some difficult life questions:

What should I do for a living?

How do I date without getting hurt?

How do I know she is the one?

How long should we date?

What are the essential qualities needed to be successful in life?

What is love?[1] And who is John Galt?

These and many other questions came to mind as I shelved my textbooks and dragged my roller bags out of the seminary where I spent half my life.

As a Catholic, I wanted to know what my religion has to say about these concerns. That is, after all, why I am

---

[1] Apparently the most Googled question in 2011

Catholic. I don't just want to be a Catholic; I also want to try to *live* as a Catholic. I want practical tips and good advice. Does the Catholic Church have any? Are you supposed to figure out all these life challenges on your own?

The Catholic Church is more vocal about addressing life challenges than perhaps any other world religion. She publishes encyclicals, apostolic exhortations, councils, regular homilies, and discourses. She has spoken on topics ranging from social solidarity to sex, from the meaning of suffering to the theology of sacramental life. This comes through the Bishop of Rome (the Pope) with the aid of the other 5000+ Catholic bishops throughout the world.

However, anyone who has researched the topic of "bachelor" or "bachelorette" in Catholic doctrine or teachings knows the search is futile. There is plenty of literature for priests, nuns, consecrated and married people. Unfortunately, very little exists for single people.

The Vatican has not published a catechism on the single life. However, does the Church have any lifestyle advice to give in some other roundabout, indirect way? I thought back to all the Church had taught me and settled on one lesson in particular that could shed light on the subject: the experience of being a religious. By religious, I don't simply mean someone who is religious. The religious I speak of are members of a religious congregation within the Catholic Church.

These members of religious congregations have consecrated their lives completely to the church. St. Ignatius Loyola of the Jesuits and Mother Teresa of the Missionaries of Charity are two examples. They got "married" to the church. The church "employs" them. The Church is their "cause" in the way that a clinical researcher might dedicate his life to curing Asian elephants from the *endotheliotropic herpes virus.* He puts in extra hours, spends nights at the lab, talks often about his mission and is almost always thinking about a new test or approach to reach the cure. It is dedication beyond a career. It is a lifestyle. The religious live something like that. As priests, nuns, and other forms of consecrated life in the Church, they are completely dedicated to the humanitarian and spiritual mission of the Catholic Church.

The church has more to say about a religious lifestyle than it does about a married or single lay person. The Church has "control" over the lifestyle of the religious because they have dedicated their lives to the Church. She trains them in a unique way and teaches them virtues and mental habits. Their day is guided by a routine of prayers and activities from the moment they rise until last vespers.

The way the Church relates to a religious is how the Church would marry someone. They are, again, like spouses of the Church. The Church is very involved in their day-to-day life and routine. They are committed to the Church and the Church is committed to them. Consequently, the Church has more practical guidelines with regards to religious life. There are religious lifestyle traditions generated and handed down through the centuries. Some of them are unwritten, others were written and all are in some way rooted in the Gospels.

The general lifestyle guidelines the Church has for religious life become more specific in the constitutions. All religious congregations have a constitution. Whether one is a Franciscan, a Jesuit, or a Carmelite, the constitution one lives by has been reviewed and approved by the Vatican and that constitution guides their members on how to live. I wish I had a constitution for my single life.

The Church is more directly involved in the lifestyle of a religious because they are in a sense dating and eventually marrying the Church. If you are just friends with someone, you are less concerned with whether they spend their evenings watching reality shows or at spinning class. You just want to get a drink once a week and how they run the rest of their life is up to them. However, if you are seriously dating or in a relationship, you are more involved in what they do and how they solve daily challenges. That is the Church-religious relationship.

I understood this about the religious lifestyle because I was a religious for 15 years, training to be a Catholic priest. At the end of that period, my superiors told me it was time to move on and gave me two reasons why. Those reasons are a subject for another day, I won't get into that. "Religious life," they began, "is not for you." The point is I was now suddenly that single, Catholic bachelor. I had all those above-mentioned questions that single people query about life. Where? How? What? Job? Girl? Love?

In the quest for answers, I searched the Catechism of the Catholic Church, the Bible and any Catholic based materials I could lay my hands on that could be closely related to the drama of single life. I didn't find the clear, practical answers I was looking for.

Eventually, I asked myself, "What would happen if I started applying some principles of Catholic religious life to my life as a Catholic bachelor. What would happen if I dated a woman as the Church had dated me? If I trained myself in my career the way the Church trained me in religious life? What would happen if I rebuilt in myself some of the core habits of religious life in my new lifestyle as a single, young professional?

And so I started with a small, one-man experiment over a period of four years. I was the experiment. Along the way, other young Catholics, who shared the same confusion, joined me. Seeing that I was looking for answers, they approached me with their questions, and I gave them advice. It wasn't just about me anymore. Others were participating in these ideas, also.

I wrote about my experiences in a journal, and what you will read in this book are the results of that. It is a story of what happens when you apply some practical lifestyle habits of Catholic religious life to the layman's (or woman's) life.

Does it work? Will it end in a lifestyle disaster? Does the Catholic Church know anything helpful about living single, dating, careers and all the other dilemmas we hit before getting married?

1

Begin Again

*If growing up is creating ideas and dreams of what life
should be, then maturity is letting them go again.*

–Mary Beth Danielson

It all started on Valentine's Day, 2012. That was the day I
left the seminary. After 15 years of preparation to become a
Catholic priest during which I marked most days with
prayer, silence, study, and soccer, I was now out in the big
world. I was unbound from my vows of poverty, chastity,
and obedience and on my way to my first social dance.

It was my biggest lifestyle reset yet. In the space of an

hour, I went from being a seminarian to a bachelor; from being neck-deep in the biggest commitment in the world to a lifestyle of no commitment and the freedom to do anything I could afford. I actually couldn't afford to do much, but still, the idea of freedom was exciting.

I was now unattached, single, finished with school, and about to start a new career. It was the beginning of a new life. I was in a different world, and I found that the first step in this starting over was to find something to wear. I could not just go to a social dance dressed like Fr. Leo. I spread my seminary clothes out on the bed and did a quick assessment of what I had to work with.

There were black socks, black slacks, white dress shirts, and black suits. There were white athletic socks, black shoes and more black and white clothes befitting a seminarian but questionable for making an average impression at a dance. Fortunately, it was 2012, the year *Men in Black 3* came out, making black and whites cool, stylish and a bit sexy. I found some of the monocolor wardrobe salvageable and managed to put together a decent outfit.

As I sorted through the clothes, I realized that there were some items that were definitely not useful anymore, and I pondered what to do with them. The most obvious was the Roman collar.

The Roman collar is the circular black collar with a plastic white square in the middle. It is the signature clothing article for clergy, seminarians, and Catholic priests. It is what tells people from two blocks away that the man wearing it has given his life to the Catholic Church.

The first time I put on the Roman collar was 1998 when Aerosmith's 'I Don't Wanna Miss a Thing' was at the top of the charts. Ironically, I thought, from then on I would be living as a monk and missing lots of things. I would miss a generation of pop culture, music, media and whatever millennials were doing between 1998 and 2012. I am finally almost caught up on the movies at least.

I put the collar on every single morning for 15 years. It had become more a part of my life than any other thing I owned. I felt it around my neck, and I saw it in the mirror; I cleaned it daily to keep it pure white. Sometimes I loved it, especially when I strolled around the Vatican. The Swiss guards would see the clergy apparel and give a respectful, discrete salute. A few times I genuinely hated it, most especially on those summer days when it was 95 degrees at 99 percent humidity with the tight collar leaving zero space for ventilation.

As I buttoned my shirt to go to the dance, I thought about the collar. Should I put the Roman collar in a box and keep it? Should I leave it on a hanger in the closet? Or, should I just get rid of it? How much of my past should I take with me?

An experience came to mind of a younger me in a similar situation. On September 15, 1998, I was 17. I was entering a new life then, too, and I had to grapple with leaving things behind. It was my first day in the seminary. I walked through the front door and above were inscribed the words, *"Christus Vita Vestra"* (Christ Your Life). This inscription implied that your previous life, whatever it was, would be left behind. Your new life would be Christ. Welcome to the novitiate.

In novitiate, the first item on the list is inventory, the process of leaving things behind. It happens during the first week. The seminarian lays out his belongings on the bed and his superior sorts through every single thing from his tennis shoes to his wallet. Everything went into one of two piles: things that would be useful for religious life and things that would not. The "useful" pile, the seminarian, keeps. He leaves the other pile behind.

The pile to leave behind included a Nike dri-FIT polo and Russell-brand mesh basketball shorts. Brand name items were unnecessary and did not fit into the uniformity of seminary simplicity. In 1998, if that young man had a cutting edge gaming computer with 100MB RAM, that would be left behind, too. In exchange for the Nike-wear and desktop computer, he received label-less clothes and a notebook (the kind made of paper and wire spirals) to journal spiritual thoughts. The whole inventory process leaves him with nothing more expensive than a pair of slacks and nothing fancier than a Bic pen.

Possessions are just the beginning of the things he needs to leave behind as a novice. The process goes deeper: He leaves behind prejudices, dreams, behaviors, habits. He may even need to let go of small preferences for this or that food, or one sport over another. However, the process begins with the possessions.

Possessions are easily identified; they are concrete and visible. You can put them in a box and send the box away. Leaving behind possessions is very straightforward and uncomplicated. More importantly, however, possessions often carry with them specific memories that may or may not help the seminarian in his new life.

Studies show that we attach emotions to things we use and own. Sometimes we stop using things though, and they no longer have a place in our life; for instance, a pair of jeans from junior high that are now too small. We no longer use it but keep it and, inevitably, reserve some emotion for it. If the connection is significant, with time, the possession can maintain a connection to our emotions and cares, holding us back in some way from moving forward. In this case, maybe there was something about junior high that we just can not let go of—the "cool kid" drama of trying to wear the perfect pair of jeans. So we keep the jeans. In seminary lingo, we called those things "attachments," and more commonly they are referred to as "clutter" or "baggage."

If someone wants to start over without inconvenient baggage, material possessions are a great place to start.

Most single young professionals will not experience a transition like leaving lay life and entering an austere seminary. Nor will they experience the transition of leaving an austere seminary and entering lay life, but the same principle applies. Transitioning from one thing to something else is difficult often because we have neither left behind the baggage nor taken right things with us. The untrained heart doesn't know what "to keep" and "to leave" and in the struggle, it is easy to get lost and hold on to the wrong things and leave the right things behind.

Take the transition out of a college relationship, for instance. Two students meet, date, sit next to each other in class, cram exam prep sessions together; they fall in love. At the end of the school and the books, however, it is clear that they want different things in life. There is a painful break-up full of question marks and exclamation points. She's left with two things: his phone number and a valuable lesson in dating. The lesson is to talk about important plans like careers, values and lifestyle preferences, and life beyond school before falling in love. She takes one of the things and leaves the other. She holds on to the phone number and forgets the lesson. The phone number is useless while the lesson is priceless.

"Just in case," she thinks to herself. Every night and morning she thinks of texting him; and once in a while, even calling. All the while, she wonders to herself, "Why does it have to hurt so much?" as she goes through months of recovery. Why do breakups need to be so difficult? It probably doesn't help that she's holding onto something from the past, unable to let go.

"It's just a phone number. It barely takes up any space on my phone."

It is a possession that entertains a possibility that cannot be or that reminds her of a life that no longer is. So it tortures her. It is more painful to move forward when hooks from the past are pulling us back. The easiest way is to cut loose and be completely free.

It is not that most of our possessions are "bad." The

phone number is not "evil." An ex-boyfriend or girlfriend is not the enemy. It's that they are all remnants of a past that is no longer *for you*. Reminding yourself of it will not help you move on.

We accumulate things, experiences and possessions that quietly anchor us in the past, and it is difficult and exhausting to move forward. We become jaded and worn because the baggage we take with us is full of false hopes or sad memories.

All of us have that colleague in his or her late twenties or early thirties who says she's "tired" of dating; or the one who says he's "burned out" from relationships. I often believe that unneeded baggage has much to do with it. We carry it all with us, and it becomes very heavy. And in our skepticism, we forget or leave behind the good and the priceless lessons we learn from those relationships.

Sometimes we hold onto attachments with our hands if they are material; other times with our thoughts as in the case of memories. From our experiences, we indiscriminately keep all the text messages, social media connections, and gigabytes of distracting noise. We rarely hit delete. We never right click on the trash icon and hit "empty."

"I'm not that type of person," we'd all like to say. "I

don't hold on to anything from the past."

There's a simple test you can do to see if you do. Run through all the 626 photos on your smartphone.

Ask yourself, at each one, "Will this photo inspire me?"

"Will it motivate me to build a better future?"

"What is the feeling or memory that comes with it?"

"Is it positive?"

"Is this a photo I'd like to frame and put on my night stand?"

If you end up deleting a hundred or two hundred photos, you just got rid of baggage. Photos are things. Attached to every photo that you delete is a feeling or memory that you found you can do without. You can leave it behind.

If you don't have the strength to delete a single photo, there's a good chance that you are carrying around baggage you don't need; and if it is on your phone, it is probably in many other areas of your life as well. There's stuff piling up in your closet, garage, and rented storage space. It is filling up your heart, which is running out of the room because you take absolutely everything with you from the past.

I did the photo exercise myself and ended up deleting 392 photos. Most were just bad quality or out of focus; a few were meaningless, others duplicates. Some were of past dates I didn't need to immortalize with digital images. Whatever the case, they were possessions from the past that I didn't need for the future. They didn't help me. I deleted them and treasured the few excellent photos I was left with all the more. They were the ones I'd be proud to show a friend; the ones I'd want to look at years down the road.

Possessions can affect not only our relationships but our ability to make new friends, start a new job or even just move to a new city. We're always subconsciously or consciously tied to memories of things that used to be. What should be a "happy" hour, ends up being a complaint session to a friend, "I miss Seattle. I want my old apartment back. My last job had better benefits. People here don't know how to drive...."

At this point, you can probably guess what I did with that Roman collar before heading off to the Valentine's dance. That relic from the past had no place in my future. I would never use it again. I associated it with a lifestyle and set of behaviors which I didn't need to think about for the moment. I didn't need to think and behave like a seminarian and representative of a religious congregation. I didn't need to be discrete and piously recollected. I needed a new attitude and a new set of behaviors. Above all, what I needed most was to dance. This was a dance, not a retreat.

I disposed of the collar, fixed my last shirt button and headed to the social. I poured myself into my new lifestyle, and within an hour, I transitioned from a world of padded vinyl kneelers to a dance floor shaking with remixes of Pumped up Kicks and Lady Gaga.

"You're such a natural," my new friends told me. I may or may not have been a natural, but it helped that I'd left behind what I used to be and embraced my status as a single man. Of course, the attractive young ladies on the floor also gave me plenty of incentive.

Knowing what to leave and what to take became a core principle of my philosophy for further changes I would experience. Over the course of the next four years, there would be many more transitions to come. I would work six jobs to build my career from scratch; I would go on a lot of dates – a few of them with really high hopes - only to learn that I would have to move on within a week or two. I would live in places I did not want to leave, and I would move to places where I had no intention of staying. Through all my experiences, I discerned which memories and possessions would help and encourage me in the future. I took those and left the rest.

Almost immediately I noticed good results from this process, but they became most evident as time passed. At a job performance review years after that Valentine's Day dance, my supervisors assessed my work in four areas. The area in which I "exceeded company expectations" was "adaptability and innovation in the face of new challenges." I could develop new processes and leave the old ones behind; I could continually find new solutions because I was never attached to the old way. I believe the seed was sown the day I left behind my computer and video games to begin the adventure of religious life. Then, it grew on through that Valentine experience of leaving behind the Roman collar of religious life and putting on some dance floor shoes. Knowing how to take the right things and leave the burdens behind is an important step to achieving a smooth transition.

2

The Job

There is a divinity that shapes our ends, rough-hew them how we will.

–Hamlet

If life were nothing but a series of holiday parties, I think I'd do pretty well. Just dance and be friendly to people and everything will be O.K. Unfortunately, there are other things we all need: a place to live, food and a car. I, in particular, also need boardshorts and glass-bottled San Pellegrino. All of those items cost money, and money comes with that thing called a job.

"You need to get a job A.S.A.P.," my superior told me the day I left the congregation. It was at the top of a long to-do list to make the transition out of the seminary more or less smooth.

Some things in life make perfect sense but still come as a shock: like when you go on vacation, sip on mojitos for a week, get back home and try to go for a jog. *How did this happen? I'm sooo slow! I can't believe it.* It is pretty obvious how it happened. The moment I learned I needed a job was one such moment. It made sense but was still unbelievable. *I actually needed to get a real job.*

Where would I go to get a job? What job should I get? These were just a few of the questions bouncing around in my head.

The seminarian does a lot of work, but it is mostly spiritual: preaching, counseling and other forms of Christian ministry. There are five or six job descriptions a seminarian fulfills; and he never dedicates himself to anything else. Each of those jobs, spiritual direction, for instance, is directly related to spiritual things. He generally doesn't get mixed up in the careers that normal people do. He doesn't take on a part-time position as a bank teller for extra cash. He sticks to his ministerial field, and that's it.

A job in the civilian world is different. No one cares

about your spiritual insights on the job. They won't ask *why* you are working, a consistent question in the seminary line of work. There, everything was for Christ, and if you didn't do it for Him, there was no point in doing it. Now, competency will be measured by technical ability and less by your thoughts on God, faith, or life's meaning.

As I thought about how I would go about this, I went back to my work lessons in the seminary. I recalled the first few days there, and an important lesson stood out.

BOTTOM UP

The first lesson of work was to never be afraid of starting from the bottom when you need to start over. When I looked around me after a few days in the seminary, I saw that I was surrounded by an intensely diverse and talented group of men: a lawyer, ex-special-forces, a family practice doctor, a few really smart kids right out of high school, and just many good men. However, no matter how capable anyone was or where we came from, we were all put on the same list when it came to working. We were all starting over, and we were all beginners in religious life. We all had to start from the bottom.

On day one in the seminary, they tell you that you will do great things and change the world. You will study under some of the world's most talented professors. You will help build universities, preach in the high-rises, lead missions in Central America, and maybe even publish a book or two. However, you won't do any of this right away. Your main responsibility, in the beginning, is to keep a hallway clean. For about the first two years, your most glorious task will be to push a dust mop.

What about all those big jobs? They would come, but first, the seminarian will rarely even talk to anybody from the outside world. As far as careers go, he's just a janitor in a cassock. He's in charge of 50 feet of white tiles and grout. Every morning he spends half an hour sweeping it, mopping it, polishing it. On Saturdays, he'll take a little extra time to scrub dirt out of the porous grout.

There were other jobs too, of course. If he didn't get the hallway, he probably got a pair of rubber gloves and a set of bathroom stalls for his responsibility. As always, "Keep them clean, very clean." If anyone associated him with a position or responsibility, it would be "John in charge of the E hallway" or "John, the guy who washes out the lavatories." If the father superior wanted to know if John was a good worker, he would check and see how clean the area was. Welcome to the first job.

Planning for my first job out of the seminary, I hoped I

would get my dream job right away: doing something I loved doing, which I was also good at, compensated by great pay, surrounded by interesting people, never working past 5pm and weekends off. However, I also resolved that I wouldn't be afraid of starting from the bottom once again as I had in the seminary if that's what it took. Apparently, that's what it took because for my first job I was a barista.

At the onset, the barista position appeared to be a glorious gig and a real keeper. First of all, it is not too hard to get, so I was only unemployed for a grand total of 52 minutes. That was the amount of time it took to drive to the Italian café in downtown Sacramento and interview with the manager. I used to stop there, order a coffee and study theology material. Now, however, I was just looking for work.

"Yes, you can start tomorrow," the manager graciously offered. "What are you going to wear?" he asked, glancing at my seminary outfit. He graciously slipped me a roll of cash and told me to get myself some clothes.

The job also gave me free coffee in about nine different configurations, something I didn't have much of as a seminarian. Those days, I could rarely afford anything beyond a 12oz of the daily brew. As a barista, I could make myself as many $5 lattes or cortados as I wanted without going bankrupt. I was in coffee heaven.

The following day, I rode my bicycle to the café at 6am to begin one of the most exciting days of my life: my first day on a real job. Of course, there were mixed feelings. It was not the glorified career start I had imagined and over the next few months, I'd begin to experience the challenges of starting over from the bottom.

After a few days on the register, I realized I was starting from scratch. In the seminary, I had been months away from leading a parish. Now, I find myself in charge of two yards of countertop and a coffee machine. Starting with small things isn't always easy. It isn't exactly a dream come true for a guy to get a Master's degree and then work for fifty-cents above minimum wage. There's no get-rich-quick plan for being a barista. Coffee is 98.75% water, so it is really just a step away from selling water. I think even a barman pouring water would get tipped more than a coffee barista, which averages about 4 cents a cup.

The situation became more challenging when I started making Americanos for ex co-workers or people who did work for me in my past life. Yes, if you are a barista in town, you are bound to come across them.

TOO SMART

As I struggled to adjust to my new life, our café started catering some of the same social functions I used to attend in ministry. They were events I would be at if I were still in the seminary. My previous co-workers were mingling with champagne flutes in hand while I was clearing plates and handing out bruschetta.

"I'm way too smart for this job," I thought to myself as I scraped spaghetti off a nine-inch plate because someone decided he was only half-hungry.

What was the point of all that education? You can feel dumb because you've never gone to school. You can also feel dumb because you went through lots of school and now are using it to heat garlic bread and brew coffee. Out of the two, I think the latter feels worse.

Fortunately, I didn't dwell on these thoughts for more than a few seconds. The seminarian tries not to let his education go to his head. There was a humbling tradition for the day he passes his intense one-hour comprehensive oral exam and receives his Master's degree. He's sent to the kitchen to wash pots and pans. It is not a form of punishment; it is a reminder that even the well-educated need to get their hands dirty.

Scrubbing tin was not fun. Most people would prefer a

graduation trip to Thailand and a long massage, but scratching the pots puts his education in perspective from the day he graduates. Education is not the end, only the beginning.

A good education is a great start in life, but it doesn't guarantee a guy won't have to get his hands dirty; and if he does have to get his hands dirty to keep from starving or to get started then it seems insensible to let education get in the way. In the Catholic perspective, education is a tool, an instrument for fulfillment rather than the final resting place of achievements.

A man telling people which college he attended is like telling them what tools he has in his garage. "I've got the Dewalt 18v DC927 cordless drill." OK, that's nice, but we'd much rather know what he's built with the tools, "I made a dining room table out of recycled Home Depot pallets." OK, now I'm listening. What matters more is what the Catholic man or woman is doing now, at the moment, with their training and knowledge. If they are doing something great with their great education then that's good. If they are doing something mediocre with their great education, then maybe there's room for growth. And finally, if they are using their education to do the job God has put in front of them, then that's the best thing ever.

"THE JOB I HAD BEFORE WAS BETTER"

A second obstacle to starting with small things is comparing past jobs to the present. This is the uninspiring part of starting from the scratch. You start thinking about "the job you had," "how things used to be." You used to have a nice salary and now you are on commission with a handful of cold leads. You used to be in charge of a territory of four states, and now you just satisfy caffeine addictions for the courthouse across the street. You think in "what-I-had" terms.

The "what-I-had" mentality focuses on what you miss about something, and you forget why you don't have it.

"I miss San Francisco. It was such a great place for me. Now I'm in Atlanta." Well, in reality, it wasn't such a great place because you couldn't afford to pay rent and that's why you left. If it were a great place, you would still be there because that's what people do; they stay in places that are good for them.

San Francisco isn't an option for you anymore, but the options you have in Atlanta are very real ones. You can build a life, support yourself, advance in a career, meet new people and so forth.

Likewise, it also works for jobs. If you asked me which I preferred: an absolutely amazing job that doesn't exist or an

OK one that does, I think I'd choose that OK job.

The bottom rung job has its challenges, like thinking you are too smart or too good for what you do. It helps to know, however, that it won't last for long. In the seminary, we all knew that we wouldn't be scrubbing bathrooms or polishing floors forever. There was a way out if you didn't like your little janitorial assignment. It wasn't easy, but there was a good chance it would work. The way out was this: fulfill your job with perfection.

If you do small things with perfection, then, eventually, you will be given larger responsibilities.

Like most seminary traditions, there is some Biblical support for this. One instance is Luke 16:10: "Whoever can be trusted with very little can also be trusted with much." The small tasks, the mop, broom, and sponges are a good testing ground to see how you will do with more notable tasks. If you can do them well, you will be entrusted with bigger, more significant projects. The verse doesn't say exactly who would give these responsibilities to you but taken in context, it is not hard to imagine. If men do not, no worries, God will.

"Be faithful in small things..." is the blueprint for

Christian ambition. For centuries, it has been how men and women in the Church have improved themselves. John Paul II was a great pope, we all know. However, before that, he was a great bishop; before that, an awesome priest; and before that, he was an exceptionally hard-working Catholic getting his hands dirty in a stone quarry. Great people start by being great at the small, insignificant tasks.

This approach takes humility and patience, which isn't easy when we know we're capable of so much more. However, if we really want a challenge, we need to meet and conquer the ones already before us. If you want to own your own café, first, make a very, very good cup of espresso.

The time came when I wanted to move on from being a barista. I saw that unlimited, free coffee wasn't my only ambition in life. The lobbyists and administrators from the capitol building would stroll in for lunch. They'd order whatever meal they wanted off the menu. I got a 50% discount on food at the café, but buying a full-size sandwich for lunch still stretched the budget. I wanted food. I wanted to make enough money to eat whatever I wanted.

Being envious of what others have is always a bad thing. Seeing what others have and being inspired to action, however, there's nothing wrong with that.

I knew there was something I needed to do in order to

move on. I needed to fulfill my job to perfection. I wasn't doing that at the moment. On one occasion, the manager took me aside because I didn't cut the tomatoes properly for the Roman Salad. A few days later, we "had a moment" because I didn't tamp the portafilter with the correct amount of pressure.

"Just the weight of your shoulder," he would repeat, "nothing more, nothing less."

God doesn't open up big opportunities for those who neglect the small ones they've been given. Where would be the justice in that? As humble as it was, I knew there were people downtown who wanted my job. They would come in and fill out applications, and the manager would turn them down.

"We already have a barista," he would tell them; and that barista was me.

So how could I expect God to give me something better when I couldn't do the things he'd given me with perfection? He may as well take my job away and hand it over to one of the applicants.

I began to dedicate myself to the task of perfection. For two weeks, I focused on making the perfect salads and the perfect Panini. I refined my barista abilities to flawlessly dose, distribute and tamp the grounds for each shot of espresso. I ignored ideas that I was too talented or too smart for this job. You are not too good for a job until you have mastered it.

There may be more sophisticated approaches to building a career, but this seminary approach – starting small, proactively fulfilling the job with perfection – was the way I chose; and it soon paid off.

First, I discovered a lot about myself. I remember a Philosophy 101 professor telling the class that there were two ways we could learn about people: through intuition and by seeing them in action. Intuition is like a direct spiritual zip line to another person; like when a guy catches the glance of a girl across the cocktail lounge, sipping on an *Oliveto* and suddenly says to himself, she's the one, I just know it. It is quick, direct and somewhat unexplainable.

The other way, observing action, is like dating someone for 6 months; noticing what they drink, learning whether they eat hummus or cheese dip and just spending time in action. Finally, after about a hundred dinners, a thousand hours of conversation and a couple of long road trips, you realize, she's the one.

Unfortunately, few of us are really gifted at intuition. Instead, we generally rely on the long way, observing people in action. The interesting thing though is that it's not only how we get to know others, but also how we get to know ourselves.

Serving customers every day helped me to know myself. We generally don't learn much about ourselves by sitting on the couch. Unless he's Sherlock Holmes, a gentleman will learn little of the young lady sitting next to him at a coffee shop by just staring at her. Actually, it's a little creepy. He needs to break the ice, ask her to watch his electronics while he's in the washroom, start a conversation, call her the next day, take her out a few times. In the same way, we'll learn a lot more about ourselves when we take action, try new things and get things done.

Over the course of mixing Italian sodas and grilling panini, I started getting to know myself and figured out what I enjoyed doing and what I didn't enjoy doing.

I enjoyed making people smile, but I didn't enjoy spending the whole morning making lunch for downtown Sacramento. I always had a hard time making my own lunch, much less lunch for half the capitol building across the street. So, I learned I liked service, just not food service.

I noticed that I was happier behind the gelato glass than at the cutting board. When I was out front, the gelato sales always shot through the roof. At the gelato cooler, I had the opportunity to take initiative and excel in the work. I encouraged people to take free samples after handing them their lunch.

"Here, try some raspberry sorbet. It's fat-free," not mentioning that the sugar content will probably be catalyzed into fat within minutes if you don't sprint on your way back to the office.

If I smiled enough, the downtown white collars and secretaries seemed to forget about the guilty calories and the fact that the gelato was about twice the price of prime rib in weight. However, instead of twiddling their thumbs for the rest of lunch break, they ended up enjoying the colorful sweetness. I learned I was good at helping people enjoy life and taking initiative in doing so. I liked seeing people happy. That was satisfying and would later come in handy when I started my life coaching business.

This self-knowledge was more important to me than any amount of money. I knew that by knowing myself better, in particular, what I enjoyed doing and what I was good at doing, I could make better decisions about what to do for a living. There are few things worse than being at an impasse and saying, "I don't know what kind of job I want." I had been there before, and I didn't want to be there again. In addition, every day I learned something important about other people: they had trouble making decisions, too.

People walked into the shop and stared into the pastry glass. It was usually the same question; what do you recommend? And I knew they probably had no clue what they liked. If they knew what they liked, they would have asked, "Which is sweeter, the scone or the muffin? Because I like sweet, or, which is fresher? Fresh is important to me." Instead, it's just, "Tell me which is better," because they have no idea what they want.

It's fine, and even flattering, to ask a barista which pastry he recommends, but there won't always be a barista in life to give you an opinion. You have to choose what to wear. You have to choose where to work. You have to choose your relationships, and no one behind a counter will be there to say, "I've tried that one before, you should do it," "I went out with her before, great experience, go ahead," or, "No, don't buy a bungalow, everyone says it's terrible for this area."

You just have to decide on your own and accept the consequences, good or bad, of your decision. That was something I started to prepare myself for. That's another priceless lesson the coffee bar and espresso machine taught me. Start making more decisions on your own and be happy with the consequences, good or bad.

As a barista, I learned many things. I learned about

myself and the daily morning challenges people go through. The little time I spent there was an excellent investment. I recommend it to everyone who needs money, a job, and has no idea of what they want to do. Get behind a countertop, start making drinks, and talk to people.

I was only at the Italian café for a grand total of two months. Eventually, I did learn to make the perfect espresso and Roman salad. I think once I did that consistently, God thought it was time to move on and move up because things started to happen.

3

The Inspiration

If the highest aim of a captain were to preserve his ship, he would keep it in port forever.

−St Thomas Aquinas

Inspiration is the most powerful force in the world. That's because an inspiration can move the most stubborn, lethargic, inconsistent machine in the world, the human will. Take getting out of bed, perhaps the most challenging activity known to man. At times, we'd rather stand on coals than pull the covers back and step onto the floor.

However, for an inspired person, it is different. A man is inspired by an early morning coffee with someone special. A girl is inspired by a new social event she has organized with friends. When your will is complacent or lazy, the right inspiration can get it moving again. Each person needs to find that inspiration.

Inspiration can appear in a variety of ways. Often, an inspiration is a vision of how you would like to be. When I was ten, I wanted to be a rock 'n' roll pianist and play 'Johnny B. Goode' on the main stage. That was my inspiration, how I wanted to be. Because that song was an inspiration, it moved my will to do things otherwise completely impossible, like taking regular piano lessons.

I took piano lessons and practiced every day for two hours. I had my sister teach me, then I taught myself, and eventually I convinced the most well-known piano teacher in town to come out of retirement and teach me for free. Soon I was an adolescent amateur pianist. I never did play 'Johnny B. Goode' on the main stage, but the inspiration, the vision of what I wanted to be in the future still moved me to improve myself and become something new.

After the seminary, I was older and trying to develop a career as a single professional. Once again, I found inspiration to be a powerful force. My seminary superiors were no longer around to flip on the lights at 5:30am or mentor me to greatness. I was motivated by myself and my inspirations, and if I didn't have inspiration, it was just me, which was no fun at all. In the quest to move up, make use of my talents and improve my situation, I needed to get really excited about something.

By February 2012, I began to feel that I wanted more. I started to see exactly the type of lifestyle I wanted. First, I wanted different clothes. I wore a white polo shirt and slacks to work, while businessmen walked in wearing Italian suits and cufflinks. There are few things in life that can make a man feel like a man more than a suit. The suit is the staple of manly attire. A custom suit can do more for a guy's testosterone levels than a bathtub of supplements. As I saw those suits every day, I started to feel it was time to get a job where I could wear a suit.

Then, they would toss their business cards into the free-coffee drawing jar next to the register. Each card had somebody's name on it. Seeing that day after day, I decided I wanted a job with a business card. And that was my lifestyle goal for the moment. I wanted to walk into a café wearing a suit with a personal business card in my pocket— ridiculous, but true.

However, wanting more in a career is not the same as having the courage and ambition to take the steps necessary to get it. There are many things we want in life, but only a few of them truly inspire. An inspiration is something we want more than anything else in the world. It raises goose bumps when we think about it, it makes our heart beat faster when we see it, and we feel on top of the world when we hold it. Not all the things we want in life make us feel like that. Take money, for instance. You can not just open your wallet and look at the bills inside and then be inspired. Otherwise, we'd just look into our wallets all day. An inspiration is more than just a desire or want.

As I started to open my mind to inspiration, I remembered a 17-year-old me riding a school bus, looking out the window and seeing a Ducati motorcycle on the road. That was a few months before entering the seminary, and once I entered seminary, I left that vision behind. Things are different now. Now is the perfect opportunity to resurrect the buried dream.

I went on Ducati.com to see what the machines were up to: the Monster, the Hypermotard, and the Diavel. After about two weeks of comparing styling, power to weight ratio and a dozen other specs, my mind settled on the one I wanted: the Ducati Monster. Finally, I felt inspired again, and everything became about Ducati.

With Ducati as my inspiration, I resolved to do whatever it took to get one. Once I got it, I would be completely fulfilled and happy forever, or something like that.

I took a look at my paystub from the café. After running the numbers, I calculated that it would take me about 11 years to have enough money to buy a Ducati. That meant I'd be forty-three, with two kids and a mortgage by the time I could ride the Monster 796 home. That wasn't really what I had in mind as far as inspiration. The alternative was getting a better paying job; and so that's what I started looking for. The inspiration was already changing my life.

Getting a better job, however, seemed overwhelming. There was a recession across the nation, but especially in California. For seven years, the state had been in an economic slump that cost roughly 1.3 million jobs. Many of the good jobs available were in the healthcare sector, which suffered less from the recession. At the time, I did not have any qualifications to work in healthcare, so I was—as they say in Spanish—*en la calle*.

I trusted in motivational motorcycle visions and the hope that I had been *faithful in the small things;* God would give me my break. I gave myself two weeks to find a better job. Nights were spent listening to internet radio and doing online job searches. In the mornings I went to work, and afternoons were for interviews. At one point, my older brother told me about this site called Craigslist that had job ads, so I searched there. Craigslist would be my savior.

At about the same time, I also began to share the inspiration. A good sign of a powerful inspiration is that you want to tell others about it. You share it and you are not worried about failing because the inspiration is so compelling that failure is not a conceivable option. You may, in fact, actually fail. It is just that at the moment it is inconceivable. You will tell your close confidants, your friends and maybe even people you barely know.

I remember telling an Italian customer at the café, "I'm going to buy a Ducati." Lord knows what she was thinking in the back of her mind. Probably, "Sure Barista, you can't even afford a new polo shirt." At least on the outside, she smiled and encouraged me, "Bene!"

Another time, I was sitting around a table with co-workers in the Newman Center where I had a second job. We all made ten dollars an hour and we were all sitting around a table as part of an integration activity, sharing our dreams. One girl wanted things to take off with "Brian";

another girl wanted to get a job after college; another wished for her family to be healed. I pulled up a picture of a Ducati Monster 796 on my laptop. "I'm going to get one of these," I said. It took a lot of courage to say that while working two part-time, minimum wage jobs with no benefits; but having the guts to share an inspiration is a good sign that the inspiration is real.

Now that I'm raving about an expensive motorcycle, I probably sound materialistic. I don't see it that way. In materialism, you want an excess of things simply for their own sake. The Ducati was an inspiration because it symbolized many of my cherished values: minimalism, beauty, creativity, efficiency, uniqueness. It reminded me of those values which I wanted to live for every time I looked at it. The stripped down design held together by lightweight alloys reminded me to take along only what's absolutely necessary for life and leave the rest behind. It raised my mind to higher things. Finding inspiration in evident material things is a good first step to finding inspiration in things we find hard to understand (like the Divine).

Back to the job search: About 11 days into Craigslist and my two-week deadline, I landed a position as a sales consultant at a Honda dealership. My salary was 100% commission, meaning that I could do fairly well for myself or I could starve to death. I was well aware that I'd never sold or purchased a car in my life but was willing to take the risk. I thought of 800cc of raw Italian power on two wheels and knew that this would be the only way to get it.

I walked the lot through the twelve-hour sales shifts in the California sun greeting new customers. I made dozens of cold calls every morning sourcing new clients and then several others following up with current ones. I put myself out there and learned to convince people I had never seen before in my life to spend $30,000 in 30 minutes; and, of course, to spend it with Honda rather than with Toyota across the street. I learned to negotiate deals in which everyone came out happy. None of those things came naturally to me. However, I was inspired and that's all that mattered. I didn't become wealthy, but my salary became exponentially higher than what I was making at the coffee shop.

A month later I got a business card. I wore a suit. I bought a Ducati. Then, I brought all three of them back to the café. I parked my Ducati out front, I ordered lunch from one of my former co-workers, and I tossed my card into the free coffee drawing jar. All that was to remind myself that if I ever wanted to improve my situation again, I needed only to find the right inspiration, pursue it, get married to it, stay faithful to it.

Ducati motorcycles and material things would not be the only type of inspiration I would have. A material inspiration happened to be the one that worked at that moment. There had been and would continue to be a number of other sources of inspiration: spiritual ideals, my faith, a desire to change the world, and, of course, inspiring people.

People can often be more forceful at inspiring us than material things. I think if God thought an Alpha Romeo 4c Coupe would inspire Adam more than Eve, he would have created an Alpha Romeo 4c Coupe for him instead of a woman. However, God gave Adam the greatest inspiration he could possibly give other than Himself. He gave Adam another person, a woman. Since we are all human, it's natural for us to be moved more strongly by other humans who are inspirational.

Cool toys like an Alpha Romeo or a Ducati can make for nice water cooler conversations at work, but we can spend an entire Monday day-dreaming of an amazing person we met on Friday. Then, we'll spend till sunrise talking to him or her. Inspirational people often grab a firmer hold of our lives than inspirational things.

Some time after buying my Ducati I went out with a young lady who played an important inspirational role in my life. We met at a social dance in Chicago. After successfully dancing with her twice I felt confident enough to ask her for her number. We only met up for coffee two or three times but it was enough to make an impression on me in my career path. She was a young physician starting her own practice. She pursued her career in medicine with determination and enthusiasm despite serious obstacles, not least of which, school debt. Her focus in doing what she loved reminded me of my own passion for medicine in the years before entering seminary.

However, at the time I was getting to know her, I was going through interviews with a few government agencies to become a special agent. I had given up on my medicine career, "Too old for that," I told myself. A six-month bootcamp to become a special agent I could handle. Years of schooling and residency to become a physician's assistant or doctor I could not. The idea of chasing bad guys and carrying a Glock onto a commercial flight was certainly alluring, but in spending time with her, I reawakened my passion for the healing arts. I let the special agent opportunities pass and took steps to pursue my career in medicine. Within 16 months, by God's grace, I had a job I wanted working for a medical college. I was certainly interested in going out with that inspirational young physician more than the two or three times we met up, but we were on different paths.

This is one consideration to keep in mind with inspirational people. They step in and out of your life when they want or when circumstances permit. It is rare that you will live just down the street from your favorite people your whole life. Providence seems to keep them at a distance for reasons we may never know. You have to enjoy people while they are present and let the future take care of itself. I occasionally still think about that spirited young doctor, but I have never seen nor spoken to her since. She had played her role in my life and that was it. It was a very short role, but also a positively inspirational one, to say the least.

Maybe you are looking for something more stable, lasting and dependable. There is an inspiration for that, too. That's the spiritual inspiration. The things that are spiritual last forever. Good thoughts are spiritual. Virtue is spiritual. Scripture is spiritual. God is spiritual.

On one hand, it's not easy to find spiritual inspiration because you can not simply grab the handlebars and ride 120 miles an hour. On the other hand, spiritual motivations last the longest and are most stable since they'll never rust or get dinged at the curb by amateur parallel parkers. They are confined to neither the material world nor the world of people and are more dependable than both. They are untouchable and indestructible when they are strong enough.

In the seminary days, God was my only solid inspiration for a very long time. I read Scripture and saw the things He did. He created, healed and preached; and people listened. I spoke with Him and could hear the things He wanted me to do. I contemplated God, and the inspiration grew stronger. Both during and after the seminary period, my situation changed almost constantly, but those inspirations would remain. They were spiritual.

The best part about spiritual inspirations is that no one can take them away because they are not of this world. They are in things beyond this world. No one can send a ballistic missile up to Heaven, destroy it and make it stop existing. Likewise, no one can reach into your heart and seize your spiritual inspirations; not your boss, not your in-laws, not your peers who try to one up you. Once you invest in spiritual inspirations, they are yours forever.

Inspiration of any type is good for life. Sometimes it might be a deep inspiration, one so intimate you will only want to share it with close friends. Other times it can be something more accessible, one that gets you through the day, the week, or the month. The right inspiration is the one God chooses to send your way, and I think He will always send one because the free will He gave us reaches true greatness when coupled with a great idea.

Being single and working is an excellent opportunity to generate these motivational thoughts. Generally, there is more time alone to let the mind wander and dream. It's easier to sort through these ideas with fewer outside pressures and binding obligations that full-time school or later stages of life can bring. Most evenings or days off you will have a pretty good say in exactly what you want to do, how you want to spend your time. You can take small steps to pursue an inspiring accomplishment. There are almost no limits to what that accomplishment could be. It could be to heal a broken family relationship, buy a town home, win a 10k running race, or overcome a personality weakness.

Years later, when you are no longer single, you will be satisfied that in a time of freedom, you had the guts to think a daring idea, take a chance on it, dedicate yourself to it and fulfill it.

4

Learn the Game

As long as you live, you must learn to live.

–Seneca

Early on in my bachelor days, I took ballroom dance lessons. "You don't know anything about women," a mentor told me while on the way out of seminary. "You should go take some dance lessons."

He was right. During my entire twenties and early thirties in the seminary, I remember having one full conversation with a single woman of my age. My superiors simply didn't give me opportunities to do so. Consequently, I knew very little about women. I didn't understand how they communicated. Women tell you things without reasons, and you need to figure it out. Sometimes they send messages encrypted with comments and body language. In the seminary, things were pretty straight forward. If someone wanted to sit at your table, he would sit down. If someone wanted to join your soccer game, he would simply ask. If you wanted to take vows, you said so. Once I started taking dance classes, however, it was evident that the world of women was very different.

There was one girl, a Czech, slender, tall in my beginner group whom I chatted with occasionally. One day we were paired up for the waltz. As we waltzed around the edge of the dance floor, we started talking. The first time around the floor she let slip that she was breaking up with her boyfriend. Then, the second time around she mentioned I should come out and dance salsa with her and her friends, which I found confusing since we were dancing the waltz at the moment and here she was talking about salsa. In addition, I'd only completed one introductory lesson on salsa. Why would I want to go out dancing with her and her friends in public? Anyway, I made an excuse and let it drop.

I related the conversation to a buddy a few weeks later, and he said without hesitation, "She liked you. She wanted to get to know you." I thought he was a mind reader to come to such a definite conclusion. I couldn't believe I'd missed out on a good opportunity. And so it was that I learned I had a lot to learn about romantic relationships. I was ignorant of everything that should take place between meeting somebody and rocking the first date.

It is common in your twenties and some of your thirties to be confronted with lifestyle challenges and not know what to do. As much as you would like to believe you are an adult, you are still growing up. You are still learning. It brings to mind an Instagram post I see circulated frequently: *I whisper "What the...!" to myself at least 20 times a day.* And then, I see the 22,005 Instagram millennials who liked and agreed with the post. Life today can be confusing.

Romantic relationships are no exception. Confusion is common. It doesn't help that the nature of our romantic relationships changes with age the longer we're single. You don't date when you are thirty the same way you did when you were sixteen. You are constantly learning, adapting, changing. You are constantly in situations of "I don't understand" or "I don't know what the best thing to do is."

Fortunately, I had been faced with this situation earlier in the seminary. Within those Catholic walls, I was confronted with an embarrassing "I don't know how" situation when I had to learn public speaking. Public speaking in seminary is like math in engineering school. There is no way you will get out of it.

My lack of public speaking ability became a revelation at my first rhetoric competition. I stood up in front of the class to recite some Julius Caesar from memory and nearly had a nervous breakdown. I didn't even reach the top ten in a class of twenty-five. I came out average at the very best and most likely below average. Subsequently, every time I approached the podium, my voice dropped a few octaves, my hands shook, I would start to implode, and the whole thing became very, very awkward.

Other than occasional practice sessions in class, I didn't have a lot of opportunities to speak in public. I was in school, and we didn't have any public speaking events on the horizon. However, seminary taught me two other ways to become proficient in a less embarrassing manner.

THE BOOK

The first way to proficiency is to read *a ton*. Books and study have for a long time been a part of Catholic culture.

From the earliest times, monasteries devoutly preserved classical writings and manuscripts, or "books," as we might call them today.

After the fall of the Roman Empire, there followed a period of cultural chaos in which ancient Greek and Roman and Judeo-Christian cultures were at risk of being lost. For several centuries, monasteries were a safe haven for not only biblical but also philosophical and secular writings amidst the political instability that filled Medieval Europe. Their dedication to preserving the manuscripts was documented by their patient and unrelenting efforts to copy them all *by hand*. The monks loved books.

Eventually, the first European universities sprang from the writings preserved by the monks once European societies could learn to stop fighting and dedicate some time to learning. That was the culture passed on to me in seminary, where men carried books under their arm as often as millennials hold cell phones in their hands. If there were two minutes of downtime waiting for a class to start or a few moments of standing in a line, you could be sure that nine times out of ten, a seminarian would use the opportunity to read a page or two.

There was a sense of voracious learning in hopes that reading was the first step to dominating any unfamiliar topic. This was the approach I took when I wanted to pass from asphyxiated speaker into an amateur rhetorician. I took it upon myself to read and dominate that unfamiliar field. I attacked books. Over the course of two years, I read every single book in the seminary library that had to do with rhetoric and public speaking. I started with Aristotle's *Rhetoric* and anecdotes of Demosthenes and proceeded through more modern works like Dale Carnegie's *The Art of Public Speaking* and Peggy Noonan's *On Speaking Well*. When I finished all the books at the seminary library, I walked down the path to the university library and checked out every book there, too.

At the end of it there were no more books to read on public speaking, so I organized and compiled my favorite ideas and wrote what I considered as my own manual for a Catholic rhetorician. That manual is now on a 10 MB flash drive somewhere in Italy, but the ideas are still in my head and the experiences remain with me.

Years later, after leaving seminary, I gave a dating talk for a *Theology on Tap* series. After the talk, someone came up to me and told me, "You are a really good speaker. Do you speak for these events a lot?" It was my first time speaking on that topic of dating. Mostly I've just read a lot of books about speaking.

If rhetoric could have helped with romance, there wouldn't have been a problem. If only my skills at speaking platonically to a hundred people would help me in speaking romantically to one person; but no, I would have to learn gentleman talk the same way I'd learned public speaking. I would have to start from the beginning.

Once again, I went to the library to research the topic of dating and communication. I read every book and magazine I could find worth reading. I didn't expect to become an "expert" on the topic. I just wanted to know enough to be able to ask a girl out and make it through a first date without embarrassing myself or boring her to death. Surprisingly, I found there's quite a bit a man or woman can learn about from books.

Some things are more conventional. For instance, a guy can learn that if he's going to approach a group of young ladies at a bar, he has a greater chance of building interest if he starts by asking their opinion on some intriguing topic than by trying to bribe them with drinks. There are also more serious relationship topics one can confront in books. A girl can learn from reading that Mr. Good Enough may actually make her happy or happier than Mr. Perfect.[2] That

---

[2] Gottlieb, Lori. *Marry Him: The case for Settling for Mr. Good Enough.*

could save her a divorce or two. Both can learn that before you even begin dating, it's essential to have knowledge and experience of being loved by other people, family members, or close friends. In this way, they do not become immediately dependent on their romantic relationship.

Sometimes you may find dating advice that's just good for your health. For instance, if you have a one-night stand with someone, you have an 80% chance of contracting an STD. I was not too worried about that, however, I was just trying to get out of the dugout and find a young lady to walk into a restaurant with me.

Books will never replace the learning experience of actually sitting across the table from someone you are interested in. What the book can do is make your experiences less painful and more effective. Books pre-teach you, so you don't have to make so many mistakes on other people or on yourself. They are also cheaper than experience learning.

You can learn to read the signs early on that she may respect and love you. Or you can spend a few hundred dollars on her and several precious evenings only to learn that she was just passing the time and never saw a real future with you.

She can learn the heartbreak way that his vices would get between them, or she can read a few books and learn early on that the odds are against her in her quest to change him from lazy to active. Books can also help us date more.

Often I run into a smart, put-together, young Catholic man or woman who struggle to figure out why they can not even get a spark of interest from this crush or that girl.

"Am I not attractive?"

"Am I not successful enough?"

It most likely has little to do with that. When I ask, "Have you read a good book about what women want? Have you studied a little how the male brain works?"

The answer is usually, "No, of course not."

THE MENTOR

The second way of becoming proficient in the seminary was to find someone who could mentor you. Mentorship is that timeless practice of letting someone wiser and more experienced than you give you advice. The Catholic Church was built on mentorship and the idea that people with more experience, age, and wisdom know things that you may not. They will tell you when you are wrong, and you will probably be wrong. They will give you advice, and more times than not, the advice will work. That is because they have already been there or know the answer.

Jesus mentored the Apostles. The Apostles mentored the first Christians. Many of those Christians, in turn, became saints or significant figures in the history of religion. The Church takes mentorship seriously. While in the seminary, I continuously had a mentor I spoke with every week or two. There were a few moments when my mentors gave me advice that didn't work. With hindsight, I've seen that I've proved them wrong on one or two small things. That's expected, they are only human. Usually, however, spending time with a good mentor is the best investment of the day.

Of course, for the layman, there's no formal structure for mentorship. You can go through your whole life without a mentor. There is no one "assigned" to you as there was for us in the seminary. A mentor is someone you have to seek out and find yourself. How can you find a mentor?

Most likely you won't find someone who can mentor you in everything as I had in seminary. Lay life is too complicated for that. Mentors will come who can give you advice on one or a few areas: career, spirituality, dating, relationships, family, long-term goals or finances. However, if you can start by finding just one person to share your experiences with, you are doing well.

How do you find a qualified mentor? A good mentor is someone who has something you want or is, in some way, how you would like to be. If you want to own a house, find someone who owns a house. If you want to be successfully married, don't select a 50-year-old bachelor who has been through three divorces. Find someone who has maintained a commitment for a long time. He'll tell you how to build a marriage. If you want to learn how to maintain a long-distance relationship with an astronaut, find someone who is dating an astronaut. If you want to be happy, find someone who is happy to mentor you.

The best mentors will also have mentors. They know how to receive difficult advice with humility, and so they'll know what it's like to be in your place and will give advice with empathy and good intentions. Likewise, their ideas won't just be their own and about them as so easily happens with the disconnected "lone ranger" mentors. The "mentored" mentors have ideas that have been tested, proven, or handed down by other qualified men or women. Also, by constantly improving themselves through mentorship, they won't lack in fresh ideas when you come up with new challenges and dilemmas.

John Antonio

I experienced the value of a mentor from the beginning of my dating experiences. I remember one of my early failed first dates and how much a mentor was able to help. I was sitting next to a nice Italian girl in a karaoke bar. My friends insisted that I ask her out because somehow they knew she was interested in getting to know me. I didn't have a clue but I did as they said and I got her number.

A few days later, the Italian and I went out for coffee. After the coffee date, I was talking to Fr. Joe, my spiritual mentor. Before becoming a priest, he was notoriously single. Then, he was called and as a spiritual mentor of a Catholic young adult community, I'm sure he inevitably continued to hear about the young adult dating scene.

"I went on a date, but she didn't seem interested in me," I said nonchalantly.

"She was obviously interested in you. Otherwise, she would not have given you her number and driven across town to have coffee with you," he told me.

"Oh, good point."

"Did you flirt with her?"

"Did I...what?"

"Flirt."

Of course I didn't flirt. I didn't even know the definition of flirting.

My priest mentor lowered his voice, glanced at his open office door, and began, "Look, I shouldn't be the one to tell you this, but this is how you flirt with young ladies...."

After a short explanation, it became evident to me why the Italian girl didn't show any interest in me on that coffee date. I spoke Italian. How many guys can speak Italian?! It didn't matter, I hadn't flirted and that was more important.

It probably would have taken me dozens of coffee dates and several gallons of caffeine to figure that out on my own. However, I was able to fast track with a mentor. That's a more superficial use of a mentor. They are important for more serious reasons as well.

Mentors will make you older than you are without looking it. That's what everyone wants; to be old but look young. When a young woman has someone to guide her and help her make decisions, that's exactly what happens. The mentor's wisdom passed on to the mentee lets the younger woman skip across a decade of learning and become as old as her mentor. All the while, she's still living in her youth.

Imagine a twenty-four-year-old girl dating a thirty-six-year-old guy. Typically, there will be a significant gap of experience and maturity between the two. She'll make decisions like a twenty-four year old while he does so from his thirty-six years of experience. There will be moments when he says, "No that will not work, because I tried it when I was 24, 28 and also most recently when I clocked in at 32. It just doesn't work." And she'll object and persist in her way because she hasn't had that experience.

Take the same girl, but give her a mentor, someone with significantly more experience who can verify or deny what her man is trying to tell her. The girl is suddenly older and more mature in her decision-making. She won't have to experience it at 24, 28 or 32, as he had to in order to know that "it won't work." She has a mentor who has been through it who can say, "Yes, he's right," or "No, your man is wrong." If the mentor has something she wants, she'll most likely follow the older woman's advice because that advice will help the young girl get what her mentor has.

Whether a mentor is significantly more experienced than a mentee or not, there is another important vantage point that he or she has. The mentor is emotionally removed from the situation. Emotions are good. They are part of what makes us human. Through them, we can understand situations better because we can actually feel them under our skin rather than just knowing them with our mind. That's a beautiful thing when someone looks into our eyes and says, "I like you." You not only know it, but you feel it intensely.

The drawback with emotions is that they are also like unruly children. They not only help us experience a situation but can tend to exaggerate the situation as well. If something is bad, it becomes the end of the world. If something is just nice, it becomes "the whole world" to us. Raw emotions can often blow things out of proportion. It takes a consistent habit of self-reflection, discipline and good judgment to train the emotions to be real but not exaggerated. Fortunately, a mentor is emotionally removed from our situation. She/he can be objective and often help us see things in a softer light. I can't count how many dates I felt went embarrassingly wrong but a mentor encouraged me to be realistic and give them a second chance. I usually followed their advice and never regretted giving the other person and myself those second chances.

Other people, I've found, tend to go through a similar experience. The feelings can tend to weigh in on the more skeptical side as a self-protective mechanism. After a nice encounter with someone, they end up saying for almost no reason at all, "She doesn't really like me, she was just being nice because we have mutual friends," or "I don't think he thinks I'm special, I'm sure he says that to everyone."

The mentor adds balance to that. They have no need of employing self-preserving techniques; they simply see it the way it is. Whether they give you quotable wisdom advice or not, at least it's advice that's emotionally removed from the situation.

Many people struggle with dating and wonder how to navigate it well. The evidence is not hard to find. Spend an hour at almost any coffee shop on a Saturday morning and you will see guys shaking their knees off on a first date. The girl takes a bite out of her $13 plate of Belgian waffles and apparently loses her appetite in what is clearly an uncomfortable "get-to-know" you situation. He tries to keep the conversation going before the bill comes and she folds her arms wishing she went on a five-mile run instead of an internet date.

I can not help but think that if men and women made an effort to learn how relationships work, or the basics of the psychology of the other sex, they could make it a more enjoyable experience. With the increasing availability of e-content over the years, reading has gone up. However, do we read to become knowledgeable and proficient in life skills? Do we read to master a subject? Do we focus on what we want to know and go on a relentless quest for answers? Or do we skim the sensation feed and click on the headline:

CELEBRITY GETS IN SHAPE AFTER BREAK-UP!

Do we pull our life lessons out of a 14 volume sci-fi series or an academic publication?

Have you ever been so intent on solving a problem that you checked out every single book in the library that was related to it?

It can sometimes be hard to measure how our reading has an effect on our lives and if the effect is for better, worse, or neither. However, generally, your peers and co-workers will let you know. People ask advice from the capable and proficient. If people ask your advice on finances and 401K investments, that is a good sign that you have become proficient in finances. If you are into healthy cooking, they will ask you for a recipe. If you have become proficient in Myers-Briggs psychological profiles, they will ask your opinion after going on a blind date with a confusing personality.

If there is a practical life problem that seems to set you back, now is the time to hit the books and the mentors and figure it out. If it is important to you, become an ambitious learner and get to the truth of the matter. Your twenties and thirties are not a time to resign yourself to saying, "What the...?" every twenty minutes.

If the young man tells a mentor how his date went, he would probably be less likely to make the same mistakes. If the young lady asked advice from a more experienced woman, she would be more likely to recognize a good guy when she sees him.

What if they learned how to be a gentleman and or lady? Most of us would never jump into a game of cricket without first learning the basics of how to play, but many people jump into four to six dating apps really having little clue of how to show a healthy interest in someone, how to get to know someone or basic dinner and hosting etiquette.

The Catholic way is to learn from and build off those who know more or have more experience. It may happen that you will be lucky enough to turn a garage startup into a billion-dollar technology or social media megalith all by yourself without help from anyone. However, in the area of relationships at least, I have yet to meet someone who successfully navigated the scene without any help from someone wise or experienced. You can take a chance and trust that you will learn everything on your own; or you can let others help and say without shame, "I asked for help." That is how science advances. *If I have seen further, it is by standing on the shoulders of giants.*3 There is much more science in relationships than we sometimes admit.

---

3 Newton, Isaac. *Letter from Sir Isaac Newton to Robert Hooke*

Very few of us will grow to be giants in any sense of the word, but if we are smart enough, we will stand on the shoulders of people who have learned things we have not and get very much the same effect.

5

Dating Demystified

Love sought is good, but given unsought is better.

−Twelfth Night

As you may have noticed by now, when a young guy comes out of a lifestyle of poverty and chastity, there are generally two things on his mind: companionship and money. Companionship, I thought, would be easy. The career and making a living would be the real challenge. That, however, was one of the first times in my life that my intuition was absolutely, completely wrong.

Two years out of the seminary, I had already worked three jobs with ascending pay scales. In the meantime, I hadn't managed to maintain anything close to a relationship with a girl. Once I did get past the first date, I really had no idea how to proceed.

Dating was more complicated than work. With every date, I had to deliberate where to eat, what to wear, what to say and how much to spend, all the while wondering if I were really interested in that person. At the time, some unwritten dating rules seemed completely ridiculous to me, like showing interest, but not too much interest. Then, if by a miracle I could get things started, there was the question of how to keep things interesting after that. For some reason, most young ladies found me intriguing when I asked them out, but somehow lost interest by the end of the first date. What was that all about?

For all this, there was no manual of operations as there was at work. Was there any way of telling if a relationship were going somewhere, any way of knowing that there was something real there before giving all of yourself?

At first, I tried to answer these questions by stalking dating blogs and eavesdropping on chat forums. The problem, though, was that there were no definitive answers and most of the answers actually contradicted each other.

One "expert" would say, "Make a good impression, take her to a steakhouse on the first date," and then another column would say, "Just get coffee, order the house brew and split the tab."

Finally, after hours of educating myself in diverse and divergent opinions, I decided I needed a philosophy for dating. With a philosophy in place, all the practical questions can be easily approached. A philosophy has principles and principles guide action, helping you spend less time in deliberation and more time getting things done.

I took as a principle for my philosophy the idea that the end goal of dating is to have an enjoyable experience getting to know someone with the hopes of eventually arriving at a stable, loving commitment.

That is, dating should be enjoyable, not stressful or confusing. It shouldn't leave us nervous, wondering if we'll lose "the one" and be single forever because we accidently picked a two-star bar & patio for a happy hour date.

At the same time, dating eventually involves the goal of commitment. When we find something enjoyable and good, we want it to be lasting. We want it to still be there when we wake up in the morning. Love without commitment becomes hopeless, just as commitment without love is misery.

How does commitment develop? How do you avoid over-committing? How do you sustain commitment? Doesn't it get boring after a while? Once you figure out what you want to accomplish for the day, knowing how to spend your time during the day becomes much easier. In the same way, when the level of commitment is clear, everything else falls into place.

The seminary experience of commitment is significant because the Catholic Church is one of the few (or perhaps only) institutions in the world that can convince a capable young man to sell all he has and live in a relationship of poverty, chastity, obedience—and love—until he dies. Not many people become priests, but when they do, they often stick with it. Occasionally, a priest will voluntarily leave his ministry for a cute parish secretary and make the newsfeed. However, my years of ministry on the road driving across the country showed me that for every one of those, there are a hundred priests quietly doing their job in parishes across the nation. When you compare that with the divorce rate of 50% in society at large, the results are not too bad. And of my classmates who became priests, none that I know of has dishonored his commitments.

COMMITMENT IN SEMINARY

I began my exploration by recalling how I arrived at commitment in the seminary. How did I grow in commitment there?

When I started seminary, I was a hormone powered teenager who couldn't look at a girl without thinking of a number and who thought that marriage was daily physical intimacy. Naturally, I had no idea how to prepare for commitment and no idea how to keep a commitment. I thought that if a girl were pretty enough, you would just be naturally committed to her and wouldn't want to leave. You would live happily together, forever.

About a decade later, I was 27, kneeling at the foot of a marble altar, taking vows to be forever poor, obedient, and chaste. And there was no girl around, only a crucifix. How did I get there? And how did the Church convince so many other young men to do the same? What is the process? And can the same process be applied to interpersonal romantic relationships?

The short answer is this: it happens through stages. People commit through stages.

THE STAGES

A stable, loving commitment does not come all at once. It comes through stages. Each stage is different from the one before it and also more involved on two levels: privileges and commitments. Privileges and commitments go hand in hand, and this is the genius of the Catholic tradition of commitment. It's the method of developing commitment through stages and associating them with privileges along the way. In religious life, the stages of development go something like this.

"No commitment" is the beginning. That's what the Catholic Church will tell you when you step into a seminary thinking of becoming a priest. It's a test drive, just taking a look; it's your first date. You can leave after a day or you can leave after an hour if you don't like it. You have no obligation to stay.

A young man walks into the seminary with a certain curiosity but certainly not ready to commit to anything long term. The priesthood, after all, is perhaps the greatest formal commitment in the Catholic Church. The way to take the decision seriously is to begin the process with no commitment. Only then, can you fully appreciate the grandeur of giving your life away when the time comes.

Then, if the candidate is interested, he'll want to come back. There's no obligation to do so. If he doesn't come back, there are no hard feelings. He can still go to church next Sunday without anyone whispering behind his back, "Hey that's the guy who went to look at the seminary, and he didn't stay." If anything, people will compliment him for taking a chance, for exploring, for giving the priesthood a shot.

Zero commitment may sound awesome, and some people may like to stay in that state forever. However, the other side of it is that you have zero privileges. A "visitor" is the most privilege-less status of anyone in the seminary. Your name is not on your room. You have no responsibilities. You are not up at the altar during Mass. You are just a visitor who's here today and gone tomorrow.

The next step is candidacy, which lasts two to three months. It carries privileges, like being a recognized member of the community. It carries obligations, like the need to show up on time regularly to activities. You can not just do whatever you want anymore.

After that is the Novitiate which is two years. You have the privilege of dressing like a seminarian, wearing the cassock. You are a stable member of the congregation. You have the commitment of promising poverty, chastity, obedience and living the discipline of the congregation.

First profession of vows comes next. The commitment is that you are now bound by vows and not just promises. The privilege is that you are a full member of the congregation. You wear the Roman collar, identifying with the Church in public. Renewal of vows for another three years...then, at final vows you commit forever. You receive ministries like lector and acolyte, inching your way towards the priesthood.

At priestly ordination, you can do everything, administer all the sacraments. The commitment is that your life is no longer your own, you live in service of the sacraments and the Church. On almost the same day, you "lose" everything and you also receive everything.

First of all, it would be disastrous to the human race and impractical for dating couples to follow this path of 15 years of commitments broken into four or five stages to the letter. After doing that with even two or three relationships, a man or woman would already be fifty-five by the time they are married. Women would be at risk of infertility and men would throw in the towel from impatience.

The idea, though, is that commitment is learned in progression and fully appreciated when associated with privileges. Each step is a little more committed than the one before it. By advancing slowly at a comfortable pace, each stage *teaches* you to commit a little more. In this way, the relationship not only requires commitment but it trains you in the commitment.

A similar structure in dating and relationships could be something like this. Walk into the first date telling yourself, "She probably won't be the one, but I'm putting my best foot forward, and will show her a great time." Don't look for a forever love or even let it cross your mind. If you expect that person to be "the one," you will automatically expect her to commit, and commitment is not there. Focus on the moment. Only commit to learning about your date for the next hour. Her only commitment is to do the same. Listen, ask, smile, show interest and just have an enjoyable time.

With this in mind, it's pretty clear what type of activity you will do for a first date; something casual, but enjoyable. A cup of coffee or a beer is plenty. If there is no commitment, why invest? If you do not have any obligations to each other, keep the privileges minimal. Every investment—be it time, or money—will become an emotional investment also. Emotional investments, we know well, seek security and there is no security where commitment is minimal.

There may be a second date, but if there isn't, don't take it personally. A lot of capable young men visited the seminary, and few chose to stay. I'm sure Jesus was OK with that. You may be the wrong person. You may be the right person, but for some mysterious reason the other person didn't choose you. That's normal. That's just free will.

If you continue to go out on several dates, your expectations have been exceeded. At this stage, you agree to go out more regularly while keeping your options open with other people. It's non-exclusive. You might mutually agree to at least give an explanation, or a heads up if you choose to stop dating, so the other person isn't left hanging.

The activities at this stage of dating can be creative but simple, nothing extravagant. It's a time to get to know the other person, and not to necessarily impress the other person. In the austerity of the novitiate, we were just getting to know Christ and we didn't need caviar to make that happen. These initial stages are a time to show the other person yourself not what you have or your status. Let them see your creativity, your sense of humor, your values, and even a tiny glimpse of your dreams.

You do things that are enjoyable but not necessarily an investment for you. Depending on your lifestyle, it might be a jog in the park, watch the sunrise or a visit to the museums. The investment is minimal, the commitment is limited, and the privileges are few. You have the privilege of spending time together. You are trying to discover if you like the person in a variety of active circumstances.

Extravagant dating activities at an early stage, like skydiving, may detract from the person you are going out with and put too much emphasis on the exhilarating fact that you are dropping from the sky strapped to a parachute. It might make you wonder if you actually like the person or just the activity you are doing with the person. So you try to choose activities through which you can get to know one another but not necessarily bond deeply and form forever memories. Play a game of co-ed sand volleyball, yes. Set up a candlelight dinner at a five-star restaurant? If that's a big investment for you, no. There will be time for that later.

One benefit of the non-exclusive relationship is that it helps you see if you are really interested in each other before moving forward. A good initial indicator of knowing that you are interested in someone is seeing how you feel about the other person going on dates with other people. If it makes you uncomfortable or "jealous," it can be a good sign that you really like her. If it does not bother you, then you may be just more interested in her as just a friend. You enjoy spending time with her but don't like her enough to want her just for yourself. It doesn't pain you to see her with other men. She may even be just an alternative to loneliness: *I'd rather watch the new X-Men movie with Cassandra than watch it alone. Let's ask Cassandra if she wants to go out.* In that case, be friends but there's probably no point in getting serious quickly.

After getting to know each other more, you can decide if you are suitable material for a potentially longer future. You might be thinking, "This person could possibly be the one, I don't know. However, it's worth not going out with anyone else and spending time just getting to know her."

We want to try bonding more. We commit to dating exclusively, one-on-one. We share the commitment to refrain from going out with other people, so we share some privileges as well. I begin to invest more of myself. We'll go out to lunch together, happy hour. We'll enjoy a local festival, or I'll cook a meal for her at the condo. Whatever activities I choose, they are ones that are more important to me. I consider them privileges not for just one or the other, but for *both* of us.

I think it would be a privilege for us to hold hands while we walk home. So we begin holding hands when we walk downtown or other shows of open affection. And you will always remember the moment you gave up dating other young ladies and chose only the one you have now. It happened the moment you took her hand walking home one evening.

At some point, while dating exclusively, you can decide to become a boyfriend and girlfriend and the commitment increases. You are not only committed to one another as a dating couple but are also in a relationship. This relationship brings the feeling of stability with it. You've discovered each other to be marriage possibilities. At this stage, you do even more bonding activities.

I know I like her, now I want to see if I can bond with her. I introduce her to more friends and hope she does the same with me. Now things are more public, we have a place in each other's lives. It's no longer just "Kendra," it's "my girlfriend, Kendra." I get theater tickets, Broadway, a concert. We share something more than a brief hug at greeting and leaving. We've accomplished the fundamentals of "getting to know you," so it makes sense that we are moving on to bonding. We invest more of our quality time and resources. At the boyfriend-girlfriend stage, the privileges are not exhausted, though. You still reserve some for engagement.

This makes the engagement process more significant and memorable. Many cultures already do this with the custom of the engagement ring. You do not just hand someone an engagement ring while you are only dating. Nor do you give it a few weeks before proposing. You give it to them at a specific moment after she finds your QR code to a "Will you marry me?" website and says "Yes (I commit)." However, wouldn't certain bonding experiences and newly shared privileges be just as significant to the engagement process as a stone and band of metal? These experiences and privileges can be determined according to the couple's values and imagination.

Then, there is marriage. You always save at least one privilege for the last step, and once again, it should be something more than a ring with expensive rocks. This is the ultimate privilege that comes with the "ultimate" commitment—the "I do till death do us part." Of all the things you could do with someone you love, this privilege is the one you treasure the most. It is the most intimate one to you. It is the greatest thing you have to offer in a relationship. To emphasize the exclusivity, it is most likely something only you will share with that person and no one else. It won't be hard to determine that privilege; your heart will tell you what that is.

If your bank account is the closest thing to your heart and fits this description of intimacy and closeness, then signing the other person onto your Chase checking will be it. Maybe you value your personal space above all else. Then, it will be moving in together and sharing a house. Maybe it will be sharing an ice cream cone of your favorite flavor—chocolate chunk cookie dough.

That is intimate! I would never share chocolate chunk with someone unless married!

Maybe it will be another privilege and include all of the above and more. There's nothing wrong with celebrating the big day with several important, personal experiences. Whatever the principle marriage privilege is, it will be the shared experience that you treasure the most and value above all else. It will be "sacred" because it will be accompanying a sacred commitment that lasts till the end of life.

How do you know when you are ready for this commitment? You know the same way you know you are ready to move from any other stage in the relationship—you are *dying* to have it. You are dying to have that person for yourself so you move from non-exclusive to exclusive. You are dying to be able to call that person your boyfriend or girlfriend, so you move up again. You are dying to share your whole life with that person and the privileges that come with it, so you move into engagement and marriage.

If you have all the commitments or privileges at once, you may never be sure that you actually wanted it. You were never *dying* to have it. The stages approach ensures that every step forward is a step you want to take.

This may seem like a structured approach that lacks spontaneity. What do I do if I'm at the first stage, and I just feel like being spontaneous and want to skip it all and go get matching ankle tattoos in Thailand with this person? There is nothing that keeps you from doing that if you want to take the chance or just have an adventure.

The stages, however, provide a structure and having some structure actually leads to more spontaneity because we have to think and deliberate less. We can free our minds because our mind has a good idea of what is already going on. There is still plenty of room for spontaneity in words, acts of service, messages, phone calls and the variety of activities you can do at each stage.

The process of stages is not the only way of developing a relationship. The benefit of it, though, is that it clarifies what you should or could be doing at each encounter. It clarifies where you are. It clarifies where you are going and the next steps. It clarifies how much you should be bonding with each other. If done correctly it can eliminate a lot of burnout and anxiety.

It gives the will something to desire and the mind space to decide what it wants. It helps you appreciate and enjoy commitment even years later and look back with a confident smile rather than insecure regret. Activities, as material, as they may seem, also have much to do with how we persevere in love.

In the Graham Greene novel *The End of the Affair*, the writer Beatrix has an affair with Henry's wife. In an awkwardly friendly moment some time afterwards, Beatrix tries to explain to Henry why the affair ended: "I suppose...we'd got to the end of love. She could shop and cook and fall asleep with you, but she could only make love with me." Beatrix, as commonly happens in affairs, had reached an end of love quickly. There was nothing more he could do with Sarah. There was a limited range of experiences he could share with her. There was nothing to look forward to. On one hand, he had reached the climax in a relationship, sex, and physical intimacy. At the same time, he had reached an end and had nowhere else to go. He could neither advance in commitment nor privileges. A relationship, however, needs space to grow. It can not survive on one or two pleasures alone, however intense they be.

Sometimes a dating relationship can become like an affair: zero commitment, exhausted privileges, but nowhere to go. That can happen if we get carried away by affection. Most of us have experienced something like that in at least one relationship. It's only human. We let our heart get ahead of our will and forgot the role that commitment plays in developing love. However, if we want the relationship to grow into something committed and lasting it helps to give love a place to go. That's what the progression of stages does. It doesn't take a dating expert to recognize this.

I remember the first time someone came to me asking dating advice. I was working the sales lot for Honda. Bryce, a type-A alpha salesman, was also a serial dater. Through a series of dating apps he managed to be with a different girl every Friday, and sometimes Saturday also. By "with" I don't mean that they just held hands and watched the sun set. However, one Monday Bryce came into the breakroom and told us excitedly, "I've found the one!"

"I don't want to screw it up, though," he continued. "So we didn't have sex on the first date."

I was in the middle of a gulp and the stevia soda almost came out my nose.

"We just stayed up until about 1am talking."

Oh wow, he's serious.

Bryce was not religous. He was not monogamous. He was unprincipled. I was not aware of a single rule that Bryce lived by. My own sales manager, the only one at the dealership who knew I was an ex-seminarian, warned me, "John, Bryce is the devil himself and a bad influence. DO NOT go out with him after work." Bryce himself would proudly tell you all this. Despite all that, some instinct in Bryce told him that if he wanted a lasting relationship with this woman it was best not to burn through important privileges on the first night. When it came to going out with someone he wanted to spend a long time with, he was willing to take the long route. Somewhere buried deep in his erotic little amygdala was an intuition that sex was not just enjoyable but also an important privilege. As long as he wasn't really into a young lady it was fine to burn it. However, when he found someone he really liked his intuition was to slow it down and enjoy important privileges as the commitment grew. Like bricks and mortar it takes the right mix of both to build a lasting foundation. You can not build it with too much of one or the other; nor much less can you do it with only one and without the other.

For some reason Bryce asked my opinion on the whole thing. Once I could get serious and clear my drink from my nasal passage, I shared with him a crude version of my theory of commitments and privileges.

"You seem to have a lot of experience in these things," he replied. "I'll bet you're going out a lot more than me."

No, Bryce, I am definitely not.

The reality was, at the time, I hadn't even gone on a single date. I knew nothing about dating. I just knew a lot about commitment. Of course, I ignored my boss's advice and still did hang out with Bryce after work. He was fun. And I think he had a good heart.

Even with a good "plan" and approach in place, relationships will never be simple. A relationship will always be complicated because it involves the merging of two of the most complex beings of God's creation—a man and a woman. However, there's much we can do to clarify things. There's no need to agonize and deliberate over what to do for a first or second date. There's no need to wonder if you are expecting too much or not enough. You can always avoid awkward conversations about things like marriage or how much money you make because now you know exactly when such things should be brought up. It's all in a stage. The only question is which one you are in.

There is the question of what one does after marriage. How will the stages progress, then? Fortunately or unfortunately, this isn't a book on marriage. That's a topic for another time.

6

The Fight

We pray every day. We read the Bible every day, so everybody is happy.

−Manny Pacquiao

About two years into my bachelor life, I began to wonder, "Is there anything I'd like to do before I get married?" I didn't even have a girlfriend at the time, so I'm not sure why I was worried about being married. Anyway, I thought about it and realized that there was something I wanted to do: I wanted to get into awesome shape. I wanted to get into the best athletic shape of my life. I wanted to compete in a verified sport and stand on a podium with my hand held high as the winner. I didn't mean win a finisher medal or second place. I meant I wanted to *win* and be number one.

In seminary, I was in pretty good shape. I could run up and down a soccer field for a 90 minute game, and I could climb New Hampshire's 6000 ft Mt. Washington in about the same amount of time. Exercise was a big part of the routine and discipline. However, this was nothing compared to the shape I was to get in as a single man. Now I had a gym. Now I could compete. Now I would work out to train and train to win. It wasn't just about letting off steam anymore or burning off a couple frosted donuts.

I wanted to do this while I was single, because once I was married, I didn't think I could afford a babysitter every day to be at the house while I did burpees in the gym for a couple hours. I didn't think I would have the drive and passion that comes with living life like an unattached stag. Maybe I was completely wrong. I'm not married yet, so I don't know. Either way, I began to put together a plan to get into the best shape of my life.

Rather than just become a better soccer player, I decided to try something completely new with a little more risk involved. There are times when the competitive spirit wants to run with a team and share the glories or failures that come with it. That, for me, was the community in religious life. There are times when that same spirit wants to fight alone and bear the whole weight of the match—glories and failures that come with it. That's where I was at the moment. I started looking into the combat sports and settled on boxing. That would be the venue by which I would get into the best physical shape of my life. I called on Ralph.

Ralph was a boxing coach whom I'd met while racing a 10k with my sister one Saturday morning. I placed second overall, and he noticed I was in shape. He invited me to fight with his club at Purdue University. I was teaching there, so it fit well, and I could fulfill my pre-seminary dream of competing in college athletics. I woke up at 5am one morning and walked into the boxing room not knowing a hook from a jab.

I told Ralph, "I'm ready. I want to learn how to box."

"Are you willing to get in the ring and fight? Compete?" he asked me.

"Yeeaah...," I said, not because I was willing, but because I felt like it was the right answer at the time. I really had no idea of what I was getting into. I had no idea what it was like to be punched in the head 20 times in a minute. I had no idea what sore arms really felt like. Thus began a painful and rewarding journey of the toughest physical conditioning of my life.

I'm not the only one to have a plan to get into shape. Many single professionals, both men, and women, see single life as an opportunity to become fit. Athletic clubs, running groups and gyms are full of these young people wrapped in polypropylene and spandex.

I always knew that physical shape is not the only type of shape I needed to be in, nor was it the first type of shape I got in. It's nice to have a healthy rack of abs and a strong heartbeat, but there's much more to the human person than that. There are other, deeper ways to get in shape; ways that touch our personality and spirit more closely. Philosophy, experience, and learning have left me with three such ways in particular. They are core habits of fitness that make the young bachelor or bachelorette truly fit to catch most of what life can toss their way. These habits affect the rest of our lives and relationships and help us become solid regardless of the circumstance that we're in or whom we are with. They are habits that dissolve co-dependence. They make us resolved and independent in life decisions.

GET IN SPIRITUAL SHAPE

The first way to get in shape is to get in spiritual shape. Spiritual shape is the foundation for many other ways of personal development. When things are going great, we're in "high spirits." When we're down, we have a "broken spirit." The spirit is the core of who we are and also the part of ourselves that we have the most control over. We can decide how our spirit will be and no one else can tell us otherwise. The spirit can heal too. Studies in cognitive therapy[4] have shown that the spirit can often pull a man out of heartbreak better than any anti-depressant pharmaceutical.

It's not easy to measure spiritual strength. I can't measure my spiritual strength as easily as measuring a bicep after hitting a punching bag for few days. The spirit is not immediately visible. It is known by other ways. We know it through our ability to engage in spiritual acts.

It works something like this: I see a fit-looking guy walk into the boxing gym. He's my sparring partner for the day, and I know nothing about him. He looks like he's in shape, but I don't know what type of shape. I know that he has some muscle. I don't know if his cells have been

---

4 Burns, David. 1981. *Feeling Good: the new mood therapy.*

conditioned to anaerobic or aerobic activity, if his muscle fibres are fast twitch or slow twitch, etc. However, if I see him engage in physical acts, like throw three punches a second at his coach's mitts, then I know that he's in boxing shape. I know what I'm up against.

Likewise, our spiritual acts are a sign that our spirit is in shape. There are many different spiritual acts, but there is one which holds a fundamental place. Throughout history, great Catholic and non-Catholic thinkers from Aristotle to Aquinas have had a special reverence for it: contemplation.

Contemplation is like the exercise of running for spiritual development. In high school, whichever sport you choose to play, it is almost guaranteed that your coach will send you to run, sprint, or jog for conditioning. In the same way, contemplation is the basis for spiritual conditioning. It's the spiritual exercise that everyone needs to do whether they want to build the aggressive spirit of a warrior or the tempered spirit of a monk. The nice thing is, it's not hard to see if you have it.

If you can sit at home for 10 minutes in silence and just think about your day, you can contemplate. If you can spend 20 minutes in a Church praying about a Gospel passage, you are in "contemplative shape." If you can ride the hour commute home with the radio off, just thinking of how you've been blessed, then you are exercising your spirit in contemplation.

From day one in the seminary, contemplation was the staple spiritual exercise. It was the first thing the seminarian needed to learn: to pray and contemplate. Those who already had the habit of doing so before entering had it easier. The others had a journey ahead of them. For some that meditation hour was a real struggle, like running ten miles every morning when all they'd used their legs for their whole life was walk to the fridge. They would often find it difficult to sit still with their thoughts for the frequent periods of silence reserved for contemplation.

Contemplation was suitable for the seminarian because there was a lot he had to think about. The seminarian had to think about where he was going in life, what were the ideas that would help him get there, why he was going there. It was hard to get too much of it. When a man is on the verge of a big decision, like giving his entire life to God, there's always something to think about. The day was full of silence to give him that opportunity. The halls and rooms were in almost constant silence.

There were two moments during the day when he could talk: a twenty-minute break in the morning and a twenty-five minute break in the evening. If he had a good joke to crack, he'd better do it then because the rest of the day he was working in silence and kneeling in contemplation.

Contemplation is a great exercise to do at any period of life but the sooner we start, the better; no, not tomorrow, right now is fine. Before reading more, take a moment to contemplate.

Done? Wasn't too bad, was it? However, that's not how many people see it.

Many people today are out of "contemplative shape." In a series of studies done by the University of Virginia, one study, "found that most (people) would rather be doing something - possibly even hurting themselves - than doing nothing or sitting alone with their thoughts." They feared being faced with spending six to fifteen minutes alone. It appears that we not only fear loneliness, but we also prefer not to spend time just thinking. In the studies, the participants actually preferred to receive an electric shock:

The researchers took their studies further. Because most people prefer having something to do rather than just thinking, they then asked, "Would they rather do an unpleasant activity than no activity at all?"

The results show that many would. Participants were given the same circumstances as most of the previous studies, with the added option of also administering a mild electric shock to them by pressing a button.

Twelve of 18 men in the study gave themselves at least one electric shock during the study's 15-minute "thinking" period.

Apparently, the women were slightly less inclined to shock themselves. Either they didn't care too much for shocking or they cared more to contemplate.

By comparison, six of 24 females shocked themselves. All of these participants had received a sample of the shock and reported that they would pay to avoid being shocked again.[5]

Ouch, both men and women in the study would pay not to be shocked, but on the other hand, would rather be shocked than to be left alone with their thoughts.

Another study has shown that 95% of adults found time to do a leisure activity (watch TV, read...) in the past 24 hours. However, 83% of them had spent no time at all "relaxing or thinking."[6] People don't "just think" very much. They seem to be more comfortable opening apps, tapping a

---

[5] Wilson, T, *Just think, the challenges of the disengaged mind*, in *Science*; 04, Jul 2014.
[6] American Time Use Survey, Bureau of Labor Statistics, U.S. Department of Labor: www.bls.gov/tus/home.htm#data (2012)

phone screen or watching a reality show. None of those activities, however, strengthen the spirit.

"All of humanity's problems stem from a man's inability to sit quietly in a room alone."[7] Blaise Pascal believed that if we could contemplate more, we could avoid quite a few world problems. Put in a positive spin, we could say that with silent contemplation, we could also fix many personal and eventually world problems.

Traditionally, people consider talking or debating about ways to solve problems. If there's a problem, let's talk about it right away and work it out. The seminary taught me that with silence and contemplation, I could solve many problems before they needed to be brought to the debate.

I remember one of my roller coaster dating experiences. I was going out with someone I really liked, but we obviously had some substantial differences. Every week or so, there was an emotional turbulence because of how she'd hold on to me and push me away in oscillating patterns. Before really discussing it, I took the problem to contemplation. I thought about what really mattered in life and realized that a relationship wasn't everything. I realized

---

[7] Pascal, Blaise., *Pensees*

that my wounded feelings didn't really matter much in the big scheme of things.

I thought about the virtues of forgiveness that Christ had shown to people who pushed him away. I thought about how temporal emotions are, how they come and go, even the hurtful ones. At the end of my thoughts, I was calm. My painful emotions made me feel the world was upside down, but with contemplation, I could put them in perspective and realize that they were passing and finite experiences.

This leads to our second way to get in shape: emotional shape.

EMOTIONAL SHAPE

Closely related to spiritual shape and dependent on it, emotions are strong experiences you need to learn to shape and the sooner the better. Emotions can come in many forms, too many to list; but a few common ones are loneliness, depression, insecurity, anxiety and even anger ranging from a personal "grudge" to a heated flare up. If you've ever experienced any of those, you have emotions. They all need shaping or else they *take* control and you *lose* control.

How do we know when we're in emotional shape? Emotional progress isn't the same as spiritual shape or physical shape, where "bigger is better." Having big emotions means you are emotional but not necessarily that you are in emotional shape. I like to describe emotional shape in two words: "Be O.K." No matter what happens during the day, no matter who says "yes" or "no" to you, no matter what your social calendar looks like, be able to finish the day telling yourself, "I'm O.K."

"I'm O.K." doesn't mean that things don't bother you, nor does it mean that you don't feel anything. To feel nothing would be to be emotionless, not in emotional shape. There is a big difference between these.

Some ancient Greek philosophers favored the emotionless approach. In a search for happiness, they feared the power of emotion so much that they believed only a state of *ataraxia* (commonly understood as non-disturbance and indifference) could lead to happiness and tranquility. That hardly seems to be the type of society anybody today would really want to be a part of, one in which people don't feel anything or are indifferent to everything. Nor does it seem to be the type of relationship many of us would want: to be with someone who is undisturbed and untouched by whatever happens, good or bad. Can killing your emotions make you happy?

More recent science has indicated that happiness comes with something very opposite to the Greek *ataraxia*. It's precisely our ability to share emotions, empathize and feel joy and pain with others that bring us a sense of connectedness and happiness. Yes, you can even be happy feeling pain. The difference is that you are O.K. with it.

Fortunately, as overpowering as emotions can be, we also have good tools to manage them and arrive at saying, "I'm O.K." God is thoughtful and gives us the tools we need to keep it together.

Find something funny about it and laugh. There's always something to smile about in every situation, just as there is always God's presence in everything that exists.

At one point in my boxing experience, I competed for the Indian Golden Gloves. After punching out three rounds with my opponent in front of hundreds of spectators, I was determined a loser by the decision of the judges. I walked back to the lockers, the endorphins slowly began to wear off and I realized how much of a physical beating my body had taken.

I was in one of the most physically painful moments of my life. I finally noticed my mouth bleeding, my stomach revolting, my head still pounding from the hits and a heavy nausea accompanying everything. I felt like I'd overdosed on chemotherapy. I puked in the shower room, slumped down in a hallway and managed to break a smile holding up my fists for a picture; and then there was something funny.

I looked at my hands still wrapped in tape and smiled. These hands had been trained to hold gold chalices and do the healing work of a priest. Now they had become hands of a fighter, competing in the biggest boxing tournament in the state. Amidst the pain, there was something of Divine humor and irony in the whole thing. Maybe this was God's sense of humor.

Rise above the pain, see things from God's point of view and there's often more to smile about. "Laughter is the shortest distance between two people,"[8] so it has been said. I also think it is the shortest distance between man and God. If you can laugh with God once in a while you might get to know him better. You might see things from his point of view and come to accept pain more willingly.

In the meantime, my coach came by to cheer me up and told me I fought like a champion. A sense of humor also comes more easily when you are surrounded by people who genuinely care for and appreciate you.

---

[8] Victor Borge, Danish-American Comedian

THINK ETERNITY

Probably the most humorous situation occurs when someone treats the smallest things like they are everything. In reality, everything in this world is not even the beginning of anything. There is an eternity after this life and that's where things really begin. Whatever happens to you on this planet, there is always something more important. Consequently, we can laugh at things that cause us emotional distress in the same way we laugh at a broken water glass at a wedding party. There are much bigger things happening. There is an eternity, that place Catholics and many others call "Heaven."

I ACCEPT

There's another way to get in emotional shape whether or not you manage to find a sense of humor. It isn't always possible to laugh or smile. This tool is so easy; it takes just two words. When something doesn't go as planned, say, "I accept." You may not like it or enjoy it, but you can always accept it. Catholicism is a religion of acceptance.

In the Nativity story, an angel appears to Mary to tell her she will be God's mom. Mary responds, "Let it be done," in other words, "I accept" when faced with the challenge of being a virgin and an expectant mother. It was an emotionally distressing situation; she didn't know how things would work out, but she was able to say, "I accept it."

In the Mass, the priest repeats the words of Christ while holding up the blood of Christ. In the Latin, he says "*Accipe...*" (Accept, take this). That is not easy. It is not easy to accept anyone's blood, even Christ's. Apart from the obvious awkwardness of drinking someone else's blood, even under the species of wine, I simply don't want people spilling their blood for me. It makes me feel too indebted to them. Yet, everyone in the Catholic congregation is called to accept it, to take the Body and Blood of Christ at each Mass.

Saying, "I accept" in the face of a challenge doesn't preclude the idea that you may try to fix the problem or situation. It is just the first step to fixing the problem. Non-acceptance breeds only frustration and anger, which hardly puts you in the best position to remedy a situation. Acceptance unites the will to the circumstances and puts you in control. It prevents the situation from antagonizing you. You accept it, and you will calmly take care of it just as cold, blunt steal slices the mold off the cheese.

Acceptance calms the emotions, which is what we need when emotions are high. Learning to immediately say "I accept it" is one huge step towards keeping the peace.

Emotional shape is very vital in religious life because of the emotional challenges that came with the lifestyle. Sometimes, these challenges came with the vows. Trying to get the job done with the resources of *poverty* can be frustrating. An attempt to execute your master plan under the vow of *obedience* will take some self-control. The vow of chastity is a complete joke without emotional fitness. The religious won't last more than a month in that area if he hasn't gained some control over his emotions. All the while, that seminarian or consecrated member needs to maintain the peace and composure of someone whom people can trust with their intimate spiritual problems. Those are high standards.

However, the standard is no less high for the layman/lay woman. No matter what your situation in life, there will be someone depending on you to hold it together: a child, a co-worker, a client, a friend. Often, it may be someone you don't even know who watches you from a distance looking for inspiration. That happens, too.

Learn to be emotionally fit while there are fewer people in your life and while your life is pretty much still your own. The crowd will grow; you will give yourself away eventually and get someone else in return. "In all truth I tell you, when you were young you put on your own belt and walked where you liked; but when you grow old you will stretch out your hands, and somebody else will put a belt round you and take you where you would rather not go" (JN 21:18). You will be pulled in different directions in life but be prepared and you will enjoy it.

MENTAL SHAPE

Closely related to both spiritual and emotional shape is the power of the mind. *For 'tis the mind that makes the body rich.*[9] Some people may be tempted to spend hours each day building physical strength and yet neglect the mind. Zombies also have physical strength but no mind.

The mind has the awesome power of being intentional. It can envision goals, focus on them and achieve them. I practiced intentionality for years, and it has taken me decades to appreciate its power. I remember as a seminarian there were a dozen virtues I needed to achieve and just as many weaknesses to root out. I was raw, and there would be a lot of transformation necessary to become anything close to a real missionary or man of the Gospels.

The more I read the Gospels and examples of great men of the Church, the more I saw the gap between who I was

---

[9] Taming of the Shrew, Act 4, Scene 3, 169.

and who I wanted to be. It was overwhelming how much work I'd need to do. I lacked the self-discipline for regularity, the strength of will to finish, the humility to accept correction.... Seeing all my weaknesses, I realized what I needed was to focus.

Every year, I identified the virtue that I wanted the most. I set up an intentional plan of how I would overcome the weakness that corresponded to the virtue. Then, daily and weekly, I performed the acts that would help me overcome that weakness. I only focused on one work-plan for the year: one virtue, one weakness, one single way I could be a better version of myself.

The first virtue I focused on was patience. I was very impatient and it showed in my work. I was in charge of the kitchen and would become very anxious if things didn't flow perfectly. If someone sliced onions and didn't wash his knife by hand or baked rather than sautéed the chicken as I had instructed, the weaknesses of my personality became quickly apparent. The time lapse between something going wrong and my becoming upset was about 1.5 seconds. I know my fellow seminarians working in the kitchen felt it. I was a perfectionist, impatient and hard to please.

I intentionally made the decision to work on patience. For one year, I woke up every morning and prayed for patience. I examined my morning at midday and analyzed any lapses in patience. I consciously walked into the kitchen to prepare dinner and told myself I would be patient. I went to bed at night and thanked God for granting me a little patience. At the end of one year, I had grown considerably in patience. The next year I worked on another virtue and rooted out another weakness. I didn't realize till much later how much it paid off.

Sometime after leaving seminary, I had a girl over for a date, and we were cooking dinner in my condo. I had two pots: one with olive oil heating up and the other with chili in it. I asked her to mince garlic, and she did so but threw them in the chili rather than the frying pan. Without flinching, I laughed, "I already put garlic in the chili. We'll have extra garlic in the chili." In 1998, that would not have been me. I would have been annoyed, possibly upset, and would have had to take three deep breaths and mentally united myself to Jesus Savior in order to get hold of my emotions. I was surprised by how easily I dealt with the situation and began to think about the 15 weaknesses I had rooted out since then. I realized how much I had changed.

When I left seminary, I had lost everything. What I did have, however, were the 15 strengths and virtues that I had worked on, one per year. Also, 15 of my biggest weaknesses had been systematically eliminated. There were still dozens more, but it made life easier to have made progress. I was thankful that I was intentional. I identified what I wanted to achieve each year and sacrificed to get it.

Life gets complicated, even when living single and alone. If I had tried to work on every virtue in the Bible in my first year of seminary, I probably would have given up in week two. A non-intentional life is confusing. Likewise, the confusing factor is also a good way to measure how much intentionality we have.

When a friend asks me, "What have you been up to the last couple weeks?" and I respond somewhat confused, "Awe, nothing much..." I know that I have not been intentional recently. I have not been focusing on specific achievements. I've been reacting to my job or life and deep inside saying, "What the heck is happening...?"

When I'm intentional, I respond, "I've been trying to improve my mile by five seconds...I've put a little extra time in at work, hoping to be nominated for the annual staff award...I read this book about improving my conversation skills." Intentional goals don't need to be big; they simply need to be something more than, "Awe, nothing."

This is mental shape: the power to focus on one thing and achieve it. Intentionality is easier to develop when you only have your own things to worry about. The benefits go beyond simply achieving more and having the satisfaction that your life is going somewhere.

There will be times when you will have something very painful on your mind: a lost love, a teetering career, a distressed family member. If you don't want the situation to take control of your life, you will need focus. You will need to focus on what you want to achieve just for today or just for the morning. Perhaps, you will even need to focus on what you want for the next 60 minutes and leave the problem alone. If you always live in focus, it won't be hard.

There will be a time when your job will be monotonous and boring, and you will wonder where it is all going. You will sit at work staring at a computer screen, unmotivated and perhaps even bored. Only focus will pull you out of it. Focus on the twelve numbers you need to punch into the spreadsheet or the one-line email you need to send.

There will be a time when you will have a dream, a big one, which will take a long time to accomplish. It may be to write a novel or get a second degree. Along the way, there will be many temptations to spend your life in exciting relationships that go nowhere or excessive pleasures that leave you empty-handed. Maybe you will even get tired and want to give up. Focus helps you stay on the path to achieving your goal.

Finally, there will be a time when someone wonderful will want to share her life with yours but will want to know what your life is about. Only focus will enable you to tell him or her.

"I want to build an e-commerce business and work from home."

"I want to help stop human trafficking."

"I want to help pregnant teenagers give their child a shot at life."

"I want to find a new job that doesn't stress me out."

"I just want to see if I can keep a pet goldfish alive for a week."

Whatever you tell that person, just do not reply, "Hmm...I dunno." Life should always be about something. Focus.

Spiritual strength, emotional shape, and a powerful mind—spend your single life acquiring these, not stressing about school loans or collecting pennies for a down payment on a home. Focus on the types of transformation that make every day of life better.

After 9 months of conditioning and sparring with Ralph's club, I became one of the most competitive fighters in the program. Some fighters came and went, trained for a while, then took a break. Some were overwhelmed with college exams and some just decided to use the precious mornings to sleep in or recover from hangovers. However, at 33 years of age, I had finally decided to get into the best shape of my life and I wasn't about to let it go.

I signed up for my first official fight and was matched with a young 22-year-old fighter from the University of Michigan. The fight was to take place at Miami of Ohio University, and it would be the final test of whether or not I'd gotten into shape. I walked into the gym full of fighters from universities and boxing clubs across the country. I could smell the testosterone in the air. I glanced over to the far end of the gym and could see my opponent-to-be tapping mitts with his trainer. After watching a series of featherweights knock each other out and bleed faces, our turn finally came.

The dominant emotion was that of fear, but rather than think of what my opponent could be capable of I used my contemplation to relax. I had never been in this situation and didn't know what to expect. So I thought of the other first challenges things I'd confronted; leaving home for the first time at 16, taking my first vows in seminary at 19, trying to get my first job, the nervousness of my first date at

32... I thought of all the times people had told me "no" whether I offered him my resume or offered her a lunch date. I realized that being penned up in a ring for six minutes with a guy well trained to knock me senseless wasn't really anything new, nor was it the worst thing in the world.

Round one, I came out relaxed and strong and landed a lot of left hooks. I was also a little prematurely winded, but the round was mine. Then, the one-minute break in the corner. My coach holding my mouthpiece and his wife, Melissa, squirting water into my mouth while their son filmed everything on the side.

Round two, my opponent got the upper hand on me. I tripped after he landed a combination and was on the ground for a second—not extremely bad but also not a good impression on the judges. The bell rang and I was back in the corner for the final break. A lot happened in that sixty seconds.

Ralph told me a few things I don't remember and then something surprising happened. His wife, Melissa, began to speak. She looked at my face and emphatically reminded me of why I was here:

This is what you've been training for! This is what you've been working for the last 9 months! I've had men set me straight all my life but it was something else having a woman do it. She would not be the first. What was really powerful about it was that she reminded me of my goal.

This is why I woke up at 5:00am every morning. This is why I've been eating spinach salad instead of cheese curds. This is why my friends rarely see me at the bar. That's simple but at times when your head is being knocked around by 2000 Newtons of force and you are asphyxiating from adrenaline and exertion even the simplest things aren't so clear; and it's not only in boxing matches that that happens. You need to focus on your goal. You need to contemplate. You need to control your emotions of fear or anxiety. This is what being in shape is about. It often happens that in the confusion of the fight we think only of surviving and making it through the last round but we forget why we started fighting in the first place. We didn't start fighting just to survive or "not get knocked out"; we didn't graduate from school and enter the work force just to keep up with the loans; we didn't get married just to "not be lonely". We began it all to have a winning experience.

I came back and fought more confidently. I used blocking techniques Ralph had shown me only a few days earlier. I threw punches up until the moment bell sounded and won the last round. Two of the three rounds were mine now, so I walked away with my 1-0 boxing record. All that's left of that is a photo on the wall; but when I look on it I'm reminded to win in the important things also; to get in shape in the ways that really matter—spiritually, mentally, and emotionally. Physical shape is just the beginning of true fitness.

Finally in shape. Many more "fights" to come.

Conclusion

The cosmos is a diagram just beautifully bent out of shape.
Everything tries to be straight and everything just
fortunately fails.

–G.K. Chesterton

Can the Catholic Church teach me anything about living the life of a young, single professional? That was the question I asked four years ago, and my conclusion has been, yes, it can. During this time, I've applied the principles of a Catholic lifestyle that I learned in religious life, and I've seen direct cause-and-effect relationships between these principles and my ability to navigate the practical challenges of dating, career, relationships and the attempt to build a meaningful, balanced lifestyle.

The principles I practiced in the seminary have helped others, too, through my focus groups and coaching business. They have helped readers through Catholicsingles.com who have contacted me from places as far as Columbia, Spain and across the United States.

As helpful as this "inside the Church" seminary experience was for me, I certainly wouldn't recommend it for the sake of learning good habits and Catholic thought. 15 years is a long time spent simply learning to live, and there are less painful ways of attaining the knowledge I gained. Many of the principles from the seminary helped me move forward in lay life, but in the end, it's a very different lifestyle. I've had to undo some habits from seminary just as I've embraced and preserved others.

The final analysis is this. A good Catholic life is more than a principled life in which you follow rules and do things the right way. Catholicism is not about "doing things right" in order to have a good life. Nor is it about guarding a protected life and being an example of moral perfection: someone who never makes mistakes because he never tries, never falls because he never stands up, never gets burned because she rarely gets close.

No matter how well you do things, life is always messy.

There will always be a prodigal in your family or friend circle; there will always be sinners, people making mistakes with painful consequences. There will always be heartbreaks, losses and a steep fall or two in life that leave you alone, penniless or both. Reflecting on this reality, I realized the greatest lesson I learned from Catholicism actually had little to do with success or building a better life in this world.

The greatest lesson is that life is a pilgrimage, not the end. If you are successful, don't get too comfortable with where you are. If you are a failure, don't be too miserable, because all of it passes and the final goal is not to date the perfect person in the perfect way or get the perfect career or even to become a perfectly balanced human being.

The final goal is eternity, and only love will get you there. "Though I command languages both human and angelic, if I speak without love, I am no more than a booming gong or a clashing cymbal. And though I have the power of prophecy, to penetrate all mysteries and knowledge, and though I have all the faith necessary to move mountains; if I am without love, I am nothing" (1Cor 13:1-2). St. Paul knew this from the beginning.

I learned this lesson on my last day in the seminary. For 15 years, I had done things to semi-perfection. I showed up for the 6:00am bell each morning; I accomplished every task set before me; I was faithful to some very serious vows. At the end of it, it was all gone. From one day to the next, all of that became a lifetime ago and was no longer relevant to my new situation. The spot I occupied in the chapel every morning before dawn—someone else is there now. The youth groups I started are in other hands. The people I had mentored are all on their own now, building their own lives, and my name is no longer on guest lists for weddings or birthday parties.

What I was left with was my ability to love. If my experience helped me to live life with more love, it was worth it. If it did not, then it is all gone for good. It was a humbling experience and one which I offer to anyone who seeks moral perfection in danger of forgetting love. Struggle, focus, kill yourself for a cause, but in the end, relax and be at peace. For the Catholic, there is always something bigger on the horizon than simply "doing things right". There is a goal that goes beyond this world. It is love that gets you there.

About the Author

John Antonio is a men's lifestyle writer and dating consultant for Catholicsingles.com®. He has been a guest on EWTN's *At Home with Jim and Joy* show and is a member of the Catholic Speakers Bureau CMG Booking. With a master's degree in Philosophy and concentration in Ethics, he enjoys unraveling dilemmas both as a mentor and medical professional. He currently resides in Houston, Texas where he runs a medical ethics program for resident physicians in the Texas Medical Center. During his abundant spare time he is chasing taco trucks, traveling, or training to win something.

Made in the USA
Coppell, TX
14 August 2020

33209629R00080